Pocket Billiards

Exhibition by

D0916257

World Champion

NICK VARNER

──── SHOW TIME ────

PLACE:

DATE: **TIME:**

WORLD'S GREATEST TRICK SHOT SHOW

ISBN 0-9607536-0-5

Fifth Printing

© 1981 By Nick Varner
Library of Congress Catalog Card No.: 81-90170
Varner, Nick
    The World Champion On Winning
    Pool and Trick Shots
Owensboro, Ky.; Varner, N.

PRINTED IN U.S.A.

Address all correspondence to:

NICK VARNER
3721 War Admiral Drive
Owensboro, Kentucky 42303

THE WORLD CHAMPION ON WINNING POOL AND TRICK SHOTS

BY NICK VARNER

Drawings by Buddy Westmoreland
Photographs by Will Lott

Howard Cosell congratulating Nick after winning the 1982 World 9-Ball Championship at Harrah's Hotel in Atlantic City.
Mike Sigel on the left and Jim Rempe on the right are toasting Nick's Championship.

To my mother, Betty Varner, and my father, Nicholas Varner—
I dedicate this book.

CONTENTS

THE AUTHOR

Nick was born on May 15, 1948, in Owensboro, Kentucky. Raised on a farm in southern Indiana, Nick started playing the game at age five when his father bought a small pool room in Grandview, Indiana. (He just couldn't WAIT to get started!) As anyone who knows Nick might suspect, he was not a very big fellow at five years of age. So, a familiar sight in the Grandview room was Nick pulling a Coke case around the table so that he could reach the shots. His father, Nicholas, gave him constant encouragement and saw to it that Nick developed the proper fundamentals. As he grew older, Nick kept busy on the farm, but if it happened to rain, you could find him stroking balls in the pool room. Nick also took an interest in golf, and during his four years of high school at Tell City, Indiana, he was a letterman on the golf team.

Even though Nick had established a reputation as one of the better local players, he didn't bother going into the school billiard room his first semester at Purdue in 1966, figuring that a farm boy would be completely outclassed. However, one day early in the second semester, Nick strolled into the billiard room and asked if anyone wanted to play. Since the current campus champion (soon to be National Collegiate Champion), Richard Daumgarth, was standing there, Nick got a game rather easily. After a couple of hours, Nick was behind by only four or five games, even though he hadn't played any pool for four or five months. Nick began thinking, "Maybe I DO have some potential ... perhaps with some practice ..." Little did Nick know at this time that on August 23, 1980, he would rise to the absolute top of pocket billiards as "The Champion of the World."

During the next three years, Nick practiced almost every day, which resulted in his winning the National Collegiate Championship two times, in 1969 and 1970. When Nick was a junior at Purdue, Joe Balsis came to put on a show. During the game, Nick ran 58 straight balls to beat Joe 150-148. Joe remarked to the press afterwards, "Nick has a lot of potential." This win gave a tremendous boost in confidence to Nick's game.

After college, Nick began playing tournaments and exhibitions in the winter months, and in the summer he worked at Christmas Lake Golf Course at Santa Claus, Indiana, for a good friend, Larry Markos. In 1975, his brother (Steve) and father asked him to help with the family business. The small billiard room in Grandview had given way to a large family billiard room and supply store (Rack n' Cue) in Owensboro, Kentucky. Helping manage the businesses along with playing in tournaments and developing an extensive exhibition schedule (about 60 shows each year) has kept him busy since 1975.

In August of 1980, his dream came true . . . Nick won "The World Championship" in New York City. Three months later, Nick was crowned the 1980 BCA National 8-Ball Champion. Because of his outstanding record in 1980, "Billiards Digest" chose him as Player of the Year. 1981 proved to be a heartbreaker when he narrowly missed repeating by finishing second in both tournaments. However, in January of 1982, Nick captured the World 9-ball championship in Atlantic City. ABC televised the tournament on "Wide World of Sports" with Howard Cosell handling the commentary.

Throughout his journey to the top, Nick has covered all the bases in pool, from player, teacher, room owner, supply dealer, and exhibition player to writer. Bob Dickerson, a close friend of Nick's, said about ten years ago that it was "only a matter of time" before Nick reached the top. Thinking back to the time of his buddy's remark, today Nick's reaction is, "I am thankful that he was right ... it feels awfully good to be Number One in the World." Famous author, Ben Lucien Burman, probably summed it up best after observing Nick perform at the Players Club in New York, when he said, "To watch Nick Varner at a pool table is like watching a portrait being painted by Rembrandt."

INTRODUCTION

This book covers the basics of pocket billiards for the beginner and the accomplished player, too. By sharing the knowledge gained from years of practice sessions, tournaments, and exhibitions, I hope to spare the reader much time and misdirected energy in developing advanced proficiency at the game of pool.

The fundamental principles of form, position play, game strategy, as well as 76 carefully chosen trick shots, should improve anyone's game and provide opportunities to "just plain show off."

According to a recent survey, over 30 million people play pool. The reason they play is because it is fun. I know every player who reads my book will not turn into a superstar, but they can learn to play a better game.

Nick Varner

Nick Varner

WORLD CHAMPION

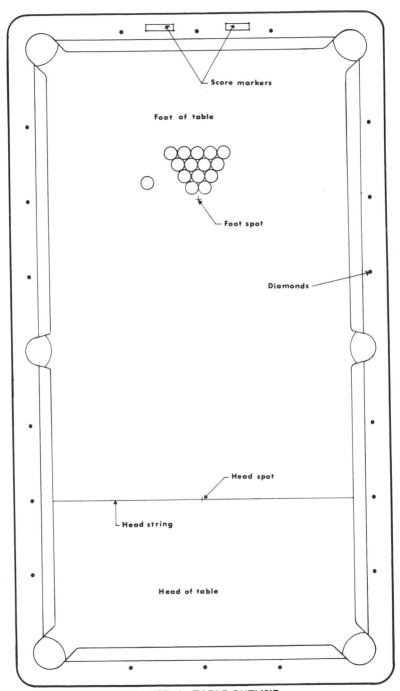

Score markers

Foot of table

Foot spot

Diamonds

Head spot

Head string

Head of table

ILLUST. 1 - TABLE OUTLINE

1

FUNDAMENTALS

Pocket billiards is no different from any other sport or game when it comes to the importance of basics. The fundamentals serve as a stepping stone from beginner to accomplished player. Often I am asked about the execution of a certain shot by a player only to find out that fundamentals are the real cause of the trouble. Good players, should they fall into a slump, constantly refer back to the basics, checking to see if they may have developed a flaw. I cannot stress enough the importance of developing good basic fundamentals.

TABLE TERMS

In Illustration 1, the table is outlined. Becoming familiar with these terms should help your progress through this book.

2

YOUR OWN CUE

SELECT YOUR OWN CUE

Many people who want to improve their pool game are under the misconception that having their own cue is an extravagance. However, if I had to play "off the wall," it wouldn't be much fun. Once you become accustomed to the feel and balance of a good cue, it will spoil you to the point that you would really hate to go back to just grabbing a cue off the rack.

To further illustrate the importance of having your own personal stick, let's assume that two professionals are playing a challenge match where one player can use his own cue and the other player must use a house stick. It would be almost a miracle for the pro using the house cue to win the match.

I have often heard people who bought their first cue remark after a few weeks, "I never thought I would say so, but I can't imagine not playing with my own cue." So why not take the plunge and find out what you are missing?

Bob Vanover, a friend of mine and a great player, was playing really well in a tournament in Chicago when a spectator came up to him between matches and asked him if he would take $1,000 for his cue. Bob said, "NO." This further illustrates the value a good player places on his own cue.

Specifications vary, but most professionals use a cue weighing between 19½ and 21 ounces, with a shaft size between 12½ and 13½ millimeters. I personally use a 19½ ounce cue with a 12½ millimeter shaft size.

CARE OF YOUR CUE

My first advice would be to not let anyone else use your cue. Unfortunately, people often do not take care of other people's property the way they should. If someone likes your cue and wants to hit a few balls to see how it feels (thinking about getting one of his own), this is fine. But turning them loose to play with it whenever they feel like it is out. Save yourself some anxiety later on by politely declining when someone wants to borrow your cue.

Next, the shaft of your cue should be kept as clean and slick as possible. Here, you have a couple of options available. First, you can spray some window cleaner on your shaft and then wipe the grime off with a clean towel. Now spray some furniture wax on your shaft and rub it with a clean, soft cloth. You will be amazed at how much slicker the shaft will be. While wiping the shaft with a cleaner gets most of the surface dirt off, eventually the chalk seeps down into the pores of the wood and you won't be able to get it all out.

The second option is easier because you just take a strip of fine sandpaper (No. 600) and rub up and down the shaft. You may see a lot of good players doing this at tournaments, because it is easier to carry a strip of sandpaper than it is to lug towels, cleaners, and wax in your pockets. Using the sandpaper does have one drawback over the cleaner and wax: it will wear some of the wood off the stick each time you use it. However, it does take a lot of sanding before you can notice a difference in the size of the shaft. The important thing to remember is to have the shaft as smooth and slick as possible so that it slides through your fingers easily.

Now, we'll move along to the tip, which is probably the most important part of the whole cue, because it is the only part that actually touches the cue ball. From my experience, I know that very few people know how a tip should look when properly shaped (Illust. 2). This is un-

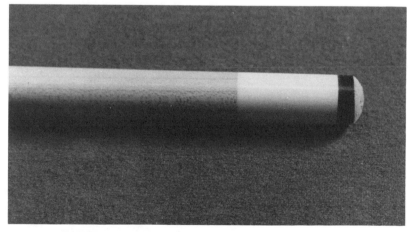

ILLUST. 2 - NICK VARNER'S CORRECTLY SHAPED TIP

fortunate, because the shape of the tip has a lot to do with your success, especially when you are hitting the cue ball close to the edges.

The tip itself should be flush with the sides of the ferrule and shouldn't overlap. Nor should it be left in its stock flat shape. You should have the tip in a smooth round knob, but don't make it too pointed (again see Illust. 2). The proper tip shape has about the same arc as a nickel. Most people use a tip trimmer and sandpaper to properly shape it.

Remember, too, that tips tend to become harder with use and from time to time they must be roughed up with a file or piece of sandpaper in order to hold chalk. The chalk should go on evenly and completely cover the surface. Dick Lane made the following statement: "I try to chalk up before I miscue rather than after I miscue." Dick's advice tells the story of chalking up.

3

BRIDGES

THE BRIDGE

You use several different bridges in the game of pocket billiards. The most important factor of any bridge is to get your hand locked into place, eliminating any movement of the hand when shooting.

The fist bridge is the easiest bridge to make. Simply make a fist with the four fingers, then put the thumb against the index finger to form a channel for the cue to slide through (Illust. 3). Plant the heel of the hand and the fingers firmly on the table. This is a great bridge for beginners.

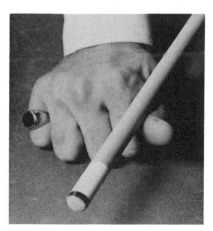

ILLUST. 3 - FIST BRIDGE - Easy to make.

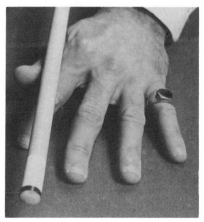

ILLUST. 4 - OPEN HAND BRIDGE - For beginners

Another good elementary bridge is the open hand bridge (Illust. 4). It is similar to the fist bridge except you spread out all four fingers, keeping the thumb against the index finger to form a channel or "V" for the cue to slide through. Apply pressure on the table with the heel of the hand and the fingertips.

After you get accustomed to one of these bridges and you would like to advance, developing one of the next two bridges is a necessity. These are called tripod bridges because the thumb, index finger and middle finger all are connected. The pressure points are the three fingertips and the heel of the hand. Basically, the two bridges are the same, except that on one bridge, the index finger is curled, while on the other (for people with longer fingers), the index finger is more on top of the middle finger (Illust. 5, 6, and 7). Notice the cue slides along the left part of the loop (index finger side). In addition, there is almost no open space in the loop around the cue. Study the illustrations closely. The tripod bridge is definitely tougher to make than the fist or open hand bridge. But the tripod bridge will give you much, much more control. **Notice the bridges of Champions:** the hand locks into place when placed on the table.

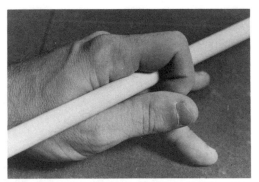

ILLUST. 5 - NICK VARNER'S BRIDGE - The shaft slides along the left side of the loop.

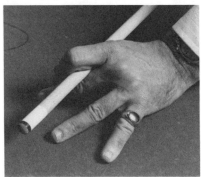

ILLUST. 6 - NICK VARNER'S BRIDGE - The heel of the hand is planted firmly on table.

ILLUST. 7 - TRIPOD BRIDGE - Index finger is on top of the middle finger.

16

SPECIAL BRIDGES

The bridges discussed so far are the ones you will use the majority of the time. There are special bridges which you must use when playing pocket billiards. First, I will show a couple of rail bridges (Illust. 8 and 9).

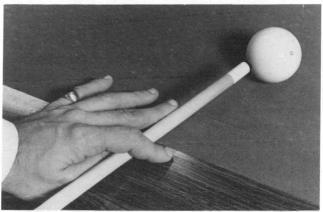

ILLUST. 8 - RAIL BRIDGE - Thumb tucked against the shaft.

ILLUST. 9 - RAIL BRIDGE - The shaft slides along the index finger.

The bridge in Illustration 8 is used when the cue ball is off the rail, but not far enough to bridge on the table. On this bridge, the thumb is tucked under and against the side of the cue. The end of the middle finger is along the left side of the cue (helping guide the cue), while the index finger is over the top of the shaft.

The second rail bridge (Illust. 9) is used when the cue ball is frozen to the rail. Study the illustration closely. You may have to elevate your cue slightly, but don't overdo it.

ILLUST. 10 - BRIDGE OVER THE OBJECT BALL - The heel of hand is up in the air.

Another special bridge is used when you are shooting over a ball (Illust. 10). Basically, it is a version of the open hand bridge with the heel of the hand up in the air.

In addition to the special bridges illustrated, there are many more that you must use. Usually they come up around the rails and pockets. Because they are too numerous to cover in this book, remember when making ANY bridge that **stability** is the most important factor. You don't want any movement in the bridge hand while shooting.

MECHANICAL BRIDGE

Having to use the mechanical bridge doesn't bring a smile to anyone's face, but sometimes you must use it. The most common mistake players make when using the mechanical bridge is holding it in the air. Simply hold the bridge down flat on the table (Illust. 11) so that, when you shoot, it doesn't move. Sight down the length of the cue to line up the shot. Hold on to the back of the cue as shown in the illustration.

ILLUST. 11 - MECHANICAL BRIDGE - Hold the bridge handle down against the table and sight down the cue.

SHOOTING WITH OPPOSITE HAND

If you attend the World Championship, don't be too surprised to see players shoot with the opposite hand instead of using the mechanical bridge, should they have a choice. Regardless of your expertise when using the mechanical bridge, you are still shooting with one hand. I can't shoot nearly as well opposite-handed. However, I can shoot better opposite-handed (using both hands) than with the mechanical bridge (just using one hand). When I first started shooting opposite-handed, I used the fist bridge. Now, I can use the tripod bridge, which helps me execute much better. Occasionally, I must still use the mechanical bridge, but learning to shoot opposite-handed has really decreased the number of times. Try using your opposite hand. After a little practice, you will develop the confidence to use it in competition. Remember: to do it, you've got to believe you can. **Think confidently!**

DISTANCE - BRIDGE HAND TO CUE BALL

The closer the bridge hand is to the cue ball, the better control you will have. The game you play most will have a lot to do with the length of your bridge. If you play 8-ball or straight pool, keep your bridge short (about 4 to 6 inches). Should 9-ball be your game, you will tend to use a longer bridge (about 8 to 10 inches). When playing 9-ball position, you will move the cue ball greater distances than in 8-ball or straight pool. Do try to stay away from bridges longer than 10 inches. If you don't, your accuracy will suffer. (Check Illust. 12). Different shots also require that you vary the length of your bridge.

ILLUST. 12 - PROPER BRIDGE DISTANCE - Guard against extra long bridges.

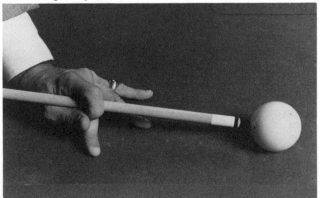

4

GRIP AND STANCE

GRIP - POSITION OF BACK HAND

"Where do I hold the cue?" Most books say hold the cue 3 to 6 inches behind the balance point. This might work, provided everyone were within 3 inches of the same height. Regardless of your height, two factors will automatically determine where you should hold the cue with the back hand. The first factor is the length of your bridge. The second factor is the position of the lower and upper arm when your cue tip is against the cue ball. Illustration 13 shows the position they should be in. Notice the upper and lower arm are close to a right angle. Guard against holding the cue too far back. Find a comfortable spot for your style and physique. Bear in mind, also, that for different shots, you will shift your grip slightly.

ILLUST. 13 - POSITION UPPER AND LOWER ARM - Almost a right angle when tip is against the cue ball.

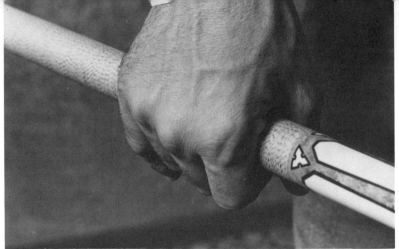

ILLUST. 14 - PROPER GRIP - Wrap your fingers around the cue so you have good control.

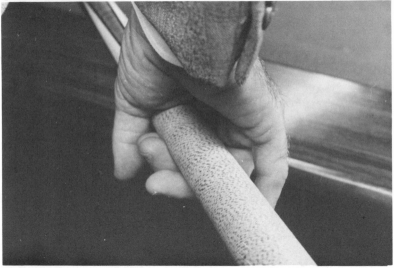

ILLUST. 15 - PROPER GRIP - Hold the cue firm enough so that you have control, but not too tight or you will lose some of the natural spring in your stroke.

Illustrations 14 and 15 show the way you should grip the cue with your back hand. For the most part, you hold the cue with your thumb and fingers. I usually let my pinky finger dangle off the cue, but you may find it easier to wrap it around the cue. If so, don't worry about it. Hold the cue firmly enough so that you have it under control. Don't clamp down as though you are trying to squeeze the juice out of it. Compare it to a firm handshake versus the one where the guy almost breaks your fingers. Study both illustrations closely, noting the position of the thumb, fingers, and back part of the hand.

STANCE

This topic is one that many players fail to realize is very important. Proper stance is crucial to both sighting and stroking the shot. The number of balls missed because of improper stance is countless.

To take proper stance, begin by facing the shot with your right foot (left-handers use left foot) on an extended line from the shot. Next, just turn your whole body 45 degrees to the right (left-handers to the left). Spread your feet apart a little wider than your shoulders. Your weight should be evenly distributed on both feet. You are now in position to drop over the cue by bending over from the waist, placing your nose directly over the shaft of the cue. Your chin will be very close to the cue, only about 3 or 4 inches above it. This is a general rule, since some players get so close to the cue that their chin may actually rub against the shaft, while others may be 6 to 12 inches above the cue. I recommend getting fairly close to the shaft because it enables you to sight down the shaft of the cue, thus aiming the shot better (Illust. 16).

ILLUST. 16 - HEAD POSITION - Get directly over the shaft and keep your front arm straight.

ILLUST. 17 - PROPER STANCE - Front leg bent and back leg straight.

Keep your front arm straight (Illust. 16). The front leg will be bent at the knee, while the back leg will be straight (Illust. 17).

The front foot will be open and about 6 inches from the extended line of the shot, while the back foot is almost at a right angle to the line of the shot. The toe of the back foot is usually against the line, sometimes slightly across the line.

You must guard against two extremes. One is the player that spreads his feet about twice the width of his shoulders. The other extreme, which I think is worse, is where the player keeps his feet close together, about 6 to 12 inches apart, which makes it very difficult to get close to the cue. You either end up standing too upright or you must crouch over the cue if you expect to get your chin close to the cue. Neither position leads to a solid, balanced stance.

Check the position of the upper and lower portion of the back arm. It should be right in line with the cue. Study all the illustrations very close-ly so that you end up with a good, sound stance.

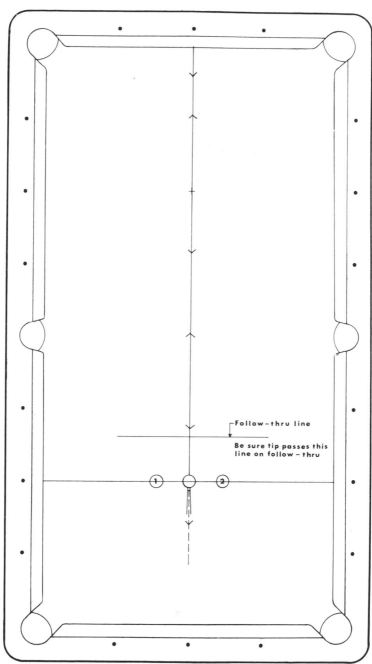

Follow–thru line

Be sure tip passes this
line on follow – thru

ILLUST. 18 - FOLLOW-THROUGH DRILL - Be sure your tip reaches the
follow-through line when your stroke is finished.

5

STROKE AND FOLLOW-THROUGH

Developing a good stroke may be the most important factor influencing your improvement. Some people do have a little more natural ability at this than others. However, if you have the desire, a good stroke can be developed. The better your stroke, the faster you will improve.

The stroke should be a fluid motion with the cue sliding back and forth in a pendulum motion. When stroking, the only part of the body that actually moves is the lower arm, although on the follow-through the upper arm and shoulder usually drop down. Guard against lifting the cue up and down like a pump handle instead of swinging it back and forth. The pump-handle stroke results from raising the upper arm. Be careful to swing the cue away from the cue ball and back without any pauses along the way. If you do pause, be sure it is at the cue ball. Before shooting, good players will swing the cue back and forth several times (maybe 6 to 8). This helps them groove their stroke. On the final stroke, you just continue on into the cue ball, letting the cuestick come to a natural stop. Normally, this will be 4 to 5 inches past the original cue ball position. All great players have one common trait: **a good follow-through.** It is hard to stress strongly enough the importance of the follow-through.

Illustration 18 shows a good drill to practice your stroke and follow-through. Hit the cue ball in the center, aiming at the center dot down the table so that the cue ball will rebound back between the two balls. If you hit the cue ball to the left or right, you won't have much luck. When you stroke the cue ball, be sure your tip stops past the original spot of the cue ball about 4 or 5 inches (Illust. 18). This will help you develop a good follow-through. Experiment, shooting the cue ball different speeds (soft, medium and hard) because you have to use different speeds when playing the game. It would be a lot easier playing all your shots the same speed, but I never said that it was an EASY game!

Try to keep the cue as close to **level** as possible on your shots. As the cue is elevated, your accuracy will go astray.

A common problem for intermediate players is position play. This, too, is more often than not a matter of **stroke** rather than strategy. Cultivate your stroke, and you'll play better position. You'll be able to control better the degree of spin and speed you use.

6

AIMING

The drill in Illustration 18 is a good aiming drill because you have to hit the cue ball in the center besides aiming at the center dot down the table. The procedure you need to use in aiming begins by picking out the spot on the ball that you will need to contact in order to pocket the ball, which may require glancing at the pocket too. You should be sighting down the shaft of the cue when picking out the spot on the object ball that the cue ball needs to hit. During your loosening-up stroking, your sighting should go back and forth several times from the cue ball, the object ball, and the pocket. Finally, when you are ready to shoot (the last stroke prior to shooting), look only at the spot on the object ball. In many ways, it is like throwing darts - you look at the bullseye, not the dart in your hand. **Remember to keep your head down on the shot and follow through.**

After shooting, many players only notice whether the ball went in or not, but if you miss the shot, learn to notice **WHY** you missed it. Did you overcut or undercut the shot? You may not have the **same** shot again. However, there is a tendency to miss most of your shots the same way. The trend is toward overcutting.

Once I asked a good friend of mine, Arad McCutchan, head basketball coach at Evansville University for many years, "When your team has a bad shooting game, what do you do?" His answer was that the following week he would increase their shooting practice time. In other words, if you want to learn how to pocket balls well...**practice pocketing balls.** Again, as the saying goes, PRACTICE ... PRACTICE ... PRACTICE ...

7

POSITION PLAY

STOP - FOLLOW - DRAW

The real key to pocketing more than one ball in a row is **position play**: controlling the cue ball so that it will go where you want it, in order to line up one easy shot after another. Many people have the misconception that professional players never miss. This is totally false. Pros miss just like the amateurs. The difference is that they don't miss as often, because by playing good position they are constantly shooting shots where the risk of missing is rather slim.

The three basic position tools are the stop shot, the follow shot, and the draw shot. Anyone can learn to execute these shots in five minutes. Picking percentages is tough, but I would say that the use of these three tools will cover 50% of the position shots you will need. This would depend to a certain extent on what game you play most often.

To make the cue ball stop after it comes into contact with an object ball, you must do three things correctly. Hit the cue ball the right speed, hit the object ball head on, and hit the cue ball a fraction below center (Illust. 19). If the cue ball stops, fine. If it rolls forward, you have hit the cue ball too high or too soft. Should the cue ball draw back, you have hit it too low or too hard. Pocket billiards is a game in which you are constantly **adjusting** and **readjusting**. Notice what went wrong and correct it. On the stop shot, as the distance between the cue ball and the object ball increases, you will have to shoot lower and harder to make it stop.

On the follow shot, speed control is a little more important than on the stop shot. Sometimes you will want the cue ball to roll forward 5 inches while the next time you may want it to roll 5 feet forward. How hard you hit the cue ball determines how far forward it will travel. To make the cue ball roll forward after it contacts the object ball, simply hit the cue ball above the center, close to the top (Illust. 20).

I have discovered that the draw shot is almost a total mystery to the average player. Good players have a tendency to favor the draw shot. Average players have trouble with this shot because they don't understand it.

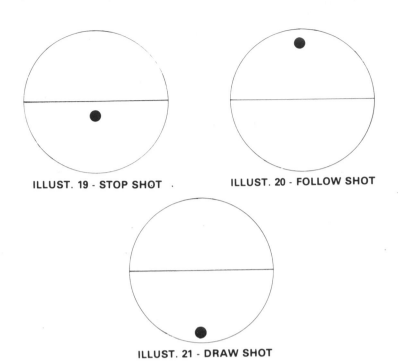

ILLUST. 19 - STOP SHOT ·   ILLUST. 20 - FOLLOW SHOT

ILLUST. 21 - DRAW SHOT

In order to draw the cue ball, you must shoot firm and low (Illust. 21). It does take more force on the draw shot than the stop or follow shot. The most common fault of many players is hitting the cue ball too high. Many times the player aims the cue tip at the bottom of the cue ball only to raise it on the final stroke. This usually is caused by dropping the butt of the cue. When the cue ball fails to come back, the player usually says, "I don't understand . . . I hit it low." The player fails to realize that the cue tip contacted the cue ball too high.

Whether you draw the cue ball back 10 inches or 6 feet depends on how hard you shoot. Again, this is called speed control, and only by practicing can you learn how hard to strike the cue ball. The draw shot becomes more difficult as the distance between the cue ball and the object ball increases, because it takes more force to draw the cue ball back. Start with the shorter shots, gradually working up to the longer draw shots. This way your success will be much greater.

At the start of this topic, I said that you can learn the stop, follow and draw shots in 5 minutes, which is correct. However, **mastering** these position shots will take a lot longer. Once you learn to execute and control these basic shots, you're on your way to playing a better game. Regardless of which shot you try, remember to "follow through" on every shot.

SPIN ENGLISH

My favorite subject in college was English ... not Chaucer and Shakespeare, but left and right English. Common among beginners is the discovery that if they stroke the cue ball close to the edge, on the left or right side, the cue ball will really do some strange things (Illust. 22).

Spin English changes:
1. the path of the cue ball
2. the path of the object ball
3. the direction the cue ball will travel after it hits the rail
4. the cue-ball speed after it hits the rail

Left and right English are difficult to use because the cue ball spins around a horizontal axis (Illust. 23). This spin is what alters the path of the cue ball toward the object ball and, after contact, changes the direction the object ball will travel. So, to pocket a ball using left or right English, you must aim at a different spot on the object ball than if you stroked the cue ball along the vertical axis (Illust. 24). If not, you are in danger of missing the shot.

Important factors to remember as you are trying to learn how to use English are ... the speed at which you stroke the cue ball, how close to the edge you actually strike the cue ball, the distance between the object ball and the cue ball, the distance the object ball is from the pocket, and how the cue ball reacts when it hits the rail.

First, the speed you stroke the cue ball, whether soft, medium, or hard, affects the path the cue ball will take. At different speeds you have to aim at a different spot on the object ball or you probably will miss the shot. Aiming at a different spot means you must adjust your aim a little to the left or right to allow for the different path that the cue ball takes when you shoot at different speeds. Many times the adjustment is very slight, but it means the difference between making a shot and missing one. If you miss a shot, you must analyze why you missed the shot (overcut or undercut) so the mistake can be corrected.

Next, the closer to the edge of the cue ball that you stroke the shot, the more spin it puts on the cue ball. Referring to Illustration 22, at different contact points on the cue ball (A, B, or C), you are putting different amounts of spin on the cue ball, which once again alters the path of the cue ball and the object ball. At the different contact points on the cue ball, you must also learn to adjust your aim on the object ball.

Third, as the distance between the object ball and the cue ball increases, so does the difficulty of the shot. If you get a chance to watch a professional tournament, you will notice that the pros will put a lot of

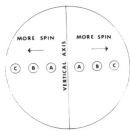

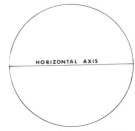

ILLUST. 22 - CLOSER TO EDGE. MORE SPIN   **ILLUST. 23 - HORIZONTAL AXIS**

ILLUST. 24 - VERTICAL AXIS

English on the cue ball when necessary. They are very consistent as long as they are close to the object ball, but as this distance increases, even the pros lose some of their consistency.

Another factor is the distance the object ball is from the pocket. The closer the object ball is to the pocket, the easier the shot. This is true whether you use English or not.

The last factor is what happens when the cue ball hits the rail with left or right English. First, it will change direction, and next, it will change speed. This is the reason that English is used to begin with. If the cue ball rebounds off the rail at a wider angle and faster speed, it is called **running** or **natural** English. Should the cue ball bounce off at a shorter angle and slower speed, it is called **reverse** English. In Illustration 25, the problem is to pocket the 1-ball and play position on the 8-ball. Stroke the cue ball with high right English. The result is that the cue ball comes off at a wider angle and faster speed (natural English). Illustration 26 shows the use of low left English, which will cause the cue ball to bounce off the rail at a shorter angle and slower speed (reverse English). Good players favor natural English. However, if necessary, they will use reverse English.

Contrary to what many players believe, pros use English to make their NEXT shot easier, not to help them make the shot. Learning to use English requires patience and practice. You must pay attention to your mistakes and learn to correct them. If you don't, you are destined to make the same errors, again and again and again.

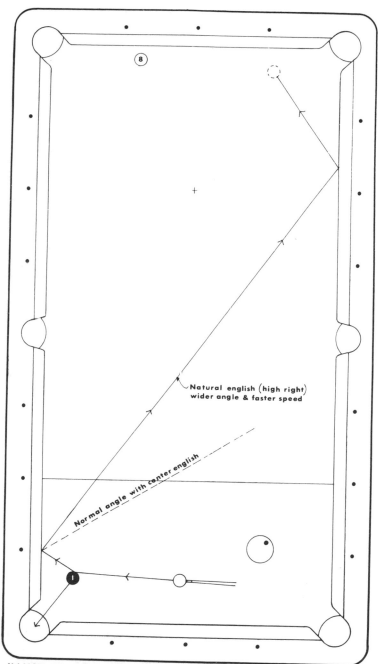

ILLUST. 25 - NATURAL RUNNING ENGLISH (High Right) - The cue ball comes off the rail at a wider angle and faster speed.

Natural english (high right) wider angle & faster speed

Normal angle with center english

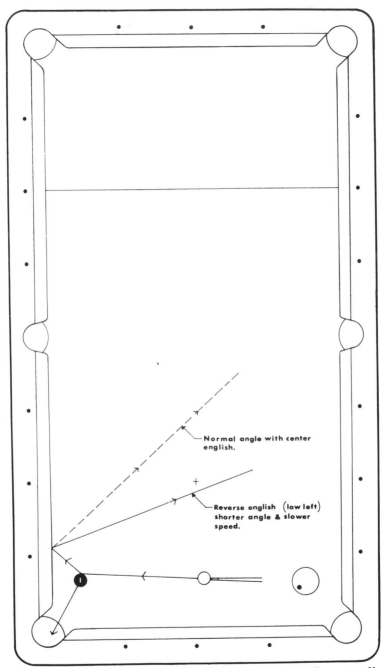

ILLUST. 26 - REVERSE ENGLISH (Low Left) - The cue ball comes off
the rail at a shorter angle and slower speed.

8

THROW, KISS, AND BANK

THROW SHOTS

Throw shots come up often both in games and trick shots. If you understand them, they are easy and can be lifesavers. I will discuss two types of throw shots, one where the cue ball and object ball are frozen and the other, where two or more balls are frozen (or very close to each other - less than ¼ inch).

The first throw shot is pictured in Illustration 27. Notice that the cue ball and the black ball are lined up along the dotted line. To make the black ball, elevate your cue about 30 degrees, aim straight ahead along the dotted line (or left of the line), and stroke the cue ball with low right English. The right English will cause the black ball to throw left along the path shown and into the pocket. By experimenting, you will find that there are limits as to how far a ball can be thrown. Two important factors in throwing a ball are the speed you shoot and the amount of English you use. The harder you shoot, the less the ball will be thrown.

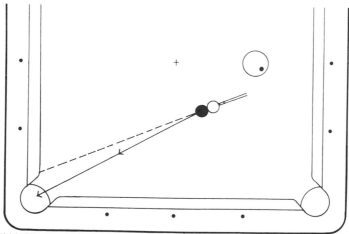

ILLUST. 27 - THROW SHOT - Be sure to elevate your cue about 30°.

So that you will never be confused, remember: if the cue ball and object ball are lined up to the right of the pocket (look at it as if you were shooting), always use right English to throw the object ball to the left. If they are lined up to the left of the pocket, the opposite holds true - use left English.

The second throw shot deals with two balls frozen together (or closer than ¼ inch apart). If the 8-ball and black ball are frozen together as shown (Illust. 28), to make the black ball you must aim to hit the 8-ball on the right side. Hitting the 8-ball on the right will change the path of the black ball so that it is thrown along the path into the pocket. Also, hit the cue ball with low left English (low left helps throw the black ball more). Again, there are limits as to how far a ball may be thrown, which you can determine only by practice. Speed is important also because the harder you shoot, the less the balls will be thrown.

Regardless of how many balls are lined up, the key to figuring out if the shot will go is where the second ball is contacted. You may hit the second ball with the cue ball or cause the cue ball to make another object ball contact the second ball. The key is contacting the second ball in the correct spot.

Once again, if the first and second ball are lined up to the right of the pocket, the second ball must be contacted to the right in order that the first ball will be thrown left. If they are lined up to the left of the pocket, the opposite holds true - hit the second ball to the left so that the first ball will go to the right. (Look at it toward the pocket.)

These shots will come in extremely handy, both in game situations and in making trick shots. Practice them so that you will have a good idea how they work.

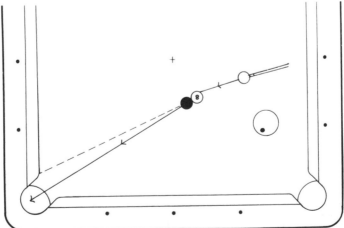

ILLUST. 28 - THROW SHOT - Aim to hit the 8-ball on the right side using low left English on the cue ball.

36

KISS SHOTS

Kiss shots are deflections off another object ball. In Illustration 29, three kiss shots are lined up. Example A is perfect because by dropping a line perpendicular to the line through the center of the black ball and 9-ball, you can see that the line goes right into the pocket. In order to make the black ball, simply hit the cue ball above the center and hit the black ball right of center. The black ball will kiss off the 9-ball and go into the pocket. If you hit the black ball too straight on and the cue ball low, the black ball might be thrown forward and miss the pocket.

Example B is a little different because, here, the line drawn between the black ball and 9-ball, bisecting the line through the center of the black ball and 9-ball, goes to the left of the pocket. If you hit the black ball more head on and the cue ball lower, you have a chance to throw it into the pocket. However, if you hit the black ball right of center and the cue ball high, the black ball will travel along the dotted line and miss the pocket.

Example C shows a shot that will not go because the bisecting line is to the right of the pocket. There is nothing you can do to make the black ball come back to the pocket. In Example B, you could throw the black ball forward but you cannot bring it back to the left of the bisecting line.

Again, practice these shots so that you understand how they work. In the trick shots and game situations, the kiss shots will prove very useful.

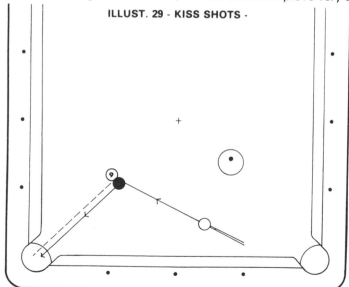

ILLUST. 29 - KISS SHOTS -

Example A — Contact the black ball slightly right of center and cue ball above center.

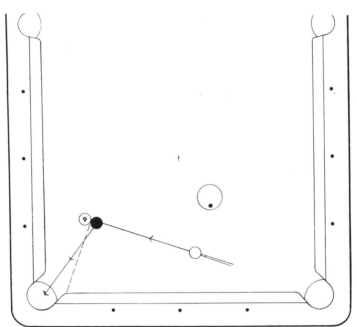

Example B — Contact the black ball almost head-on (just a fracation right of center) and the cue ball low in order to force the black ball into the corner pocket.

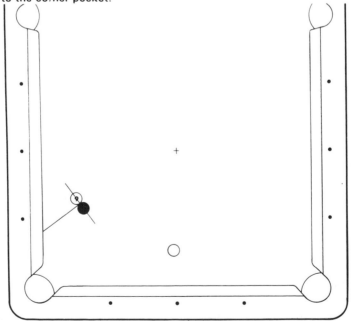

Example C — Cannot make black ball by kissing it off the 9-ball.

BANK SHOTS

Once I asked one of the best bank-pool players in the country what made him bank so well. I was hoping that he had devised a secret system which would be easy to learn. But he answered by telling me that he banked balls just like I cut them in. Through practice, he had learned to pick the right spot on the ball to aim in order to pocket the bank shot. With MORE practice, his judgment became better.

He did stress the following: whenever you miss a bank, notice whether you hit the object ball too thin or too thick. If you fail to do this, you will never be able to improve your bank shots because you won't be aware of your mistakes. The dots on the table can help your bank shots because they aid your aiming. Another important factor is to shoot bank shots firmly because they will roll truer. The real secret to banking is like the secret to pocketing balls - practice ... practice ... and more practice. Notice the drill (Illust. 30). It will help you to become a better banker.

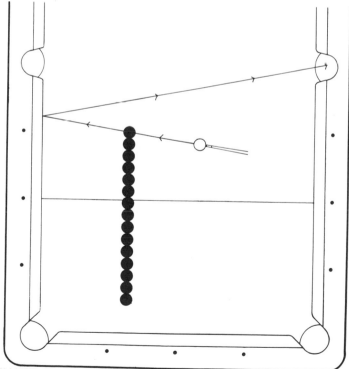

ILLUST. 30 - PRACTICE BANK DRILL - Practice banking the object balls as shown either across the side or corner.

9

8-BALL AND 9-BALL

BREAK SHOTS

A good break shot can be a tremendous advantage in any game, often either winning the game or at least putting the player breaking at a decided advantage. This holds true in reverse for a poor break shot, which usually costs the breaker the game or puts him in an undesirable situation. The next two topics will cover the break shots for 8-ball and 9-ball, which are two of the more popular games.

8-BALL BREAK SHOT

There are two different methods you can use to break in 8-ball. The first method is to put the cue ball on the headstring as shown in Illustration 31 (Cue ball Position 1), and then aim to hit the front ball **absolutely square.** Stroke the cue ball, a little below center and extremely hard, trying to make a ball on the break, spread out the balls, and leave the cue ball close to the center of the table. If you make a ball on the break, your chances of having a good shot are excellent because you have several balls from which to choose. Also, on this 8-ball break, you can try different positions along the headstring to break from, searching for the spot that brings you the most success.

The other method of breaking in 8-ball places more emphasis on making the 8-ball. Instead of hitting the front ball first, you hit the second ball on either side full and try to sink the 8-ball (Illustration 31). Because the second ball is touching the 8-ball, the 8-ball will move much more than if you hit the front ball. Thus, it has a tendency to find a pocket more often. But I must stress that the percentages for making the 8-ball on the break are still pretty low. On the smaller tables (8 foot and coin tables) you do have a better chance to make the 8-ball on the break. Since you must try to hit the second ball as full as possible, you must break from the left or right side (Cue ball Position 2) along the

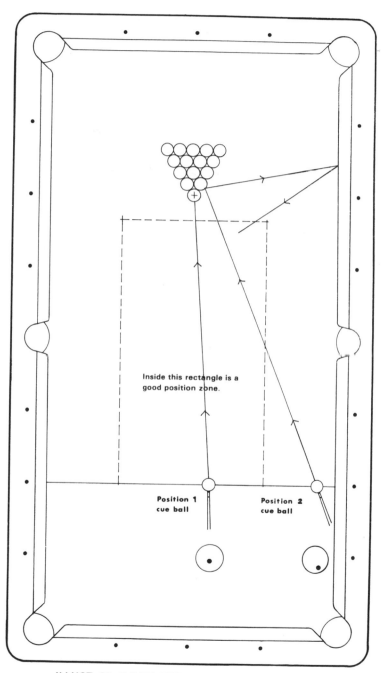

Inside this rectangle is a
good position zone.

Position 1
cue ball

Position 2
cue ball

ILLUST. 31 - 8-BALL BREAK SHOT - Two methods

headstring close to the side rail. Bridge on the side rail. Hit the cue ball with low right English (low left English if you break from the left side of the table) drawing the cue ball into the side rail so that you don't scratch in the corner pocket.

On both of the 8-ball break shots, you must hit the cue ball very hard, hopefully pocketing a ball without the cue ball scratching. If you do pocket a ball, there is a good chance that you will have a high percentage shot after the break.

BREAK SHOT - 9-BALL

In 9-ball, when two good players compete, the one with the superior break usually wins. I think the break shot in 9-ball is more important than in any other game. At times, a good break in 9-ball can prove awesome.

To break properly in 9-ball, place the cue ball along the headstring (Illust. 32). Good players vary the spot along the headstring from where they break. Often, if they don't make a ball two or three times in a row, they will move the cue ball and try a different position. They may keep moving the cue ball until a spot is found where they do have success.

Possibly the most important factor in breaking is to hit the 1-ball dead center. Hit the cue ball with a very, very hard stroke. In other words, hit the cue ball as hard as you can and still hit the 1-ball squarely. However, if you play on a lot of different tables, you will find that various tables break better when you take maybe 15 to 20% off the speed of the shot. Experiment with different speeds to find out what works best for you.

On the break shot, you want the cue ball to end up between the side pockets. This gives you the best chance to have a shot at the 1-ball. Normally, your cue will be elevated on the break shot, so when you shoot hard the cue ball will jump back from the 1-ball. Where you hit the cue ball determines what happens after it jumps back. Since you want the cue ball to stop in the center of the table, you want to hit the cue ball a little below center. If the cue ball rolls forward, then you have hit it too high, and vice versa if the cue ball draws back too far.

Many players fail to realize that the break shot in 9-ball is one of the toughest to line up. Because of the hard stroke required, if you hit the 1-ball just a fraction off center, it is going sideways, and the force of the cue ball is deflected and dissipated. You must concentrate on hitting the 1-ball **absolutely square.**

Position on the 9-ball break is so crucial because you can shoot at only one ball after the break. The break shot does tend to run in cycles.

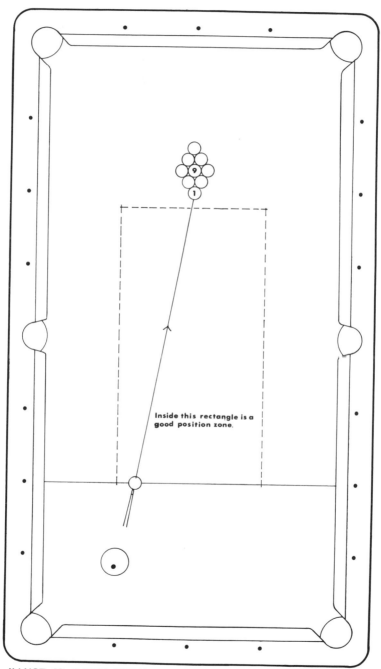

Inside this rectangle is a good position zone.

ILLUST. 32 - 9-BALL BREAK SHOT - Concentrate on hitting the 1-ball **ABSOLUTELY SQUARE**

Sometimes, you will make a ball and get straight in on the 1-ball several times in a row, while other times you will have trouble both making a ball and playing position on the 1-ball. To my knowledge, no one has the break down so well that they make a ball and get position on the 1-ball every time or even close to it. But with practice, you should be able to improve your break.

8-BALL STRATEGY

To run out in 8-ball you must learn to "think." First, you have to select which group of balls (solids or stripes) will lead to an easier run-out. Once this choice is made, you face the task of picking the order in which you play your group of balls. Hopefully your selections will result in running out your group of balls and pocketing the 8-ball to win the game.

The cardinal sin in 8-ball is to run out close to the 8-ball, failing to make it all the way. The closer you get, the tougher it will be for you to win the game. By making most of your balls, you give your opponent two advantages. First, it is easier for him to run out because your balls are not blocking his shots. Second, if he is not capable of running out, you have made it easy for him to play you safe. If two good players are playing a game of 8-ball and one player runs out close to the 8-ball failing to make it all the way, it would be a miracle for him to win the game.

The secret to playing better 8-ball is practice. With practice improvement is on the way.

9-BALL STRATEGY

To run out in 9-ball, you must learn to use your "thinking cap." Most players concentrate on pocketing the ball they are shooting and try to get position on the next ball, but only so they can pocket the next ball. In order to run out consistently, learn to play position on the next ball so you have the right angle to play position on the ball **following** the next ball. In other words, look at least three balls ahead or you will find yourself "stubbing your toe" often.

Because good players have been through so many racks, they can look at the table and size up the whole run-out in a matter of seconds. Contrary to popular belief, you won't happen to wake up one day and have it all come to you magically. It will come to you just like it came to the champions ... after **many, many** hours of practice. After a few seconds, good players can tell if the rack will be routine or difficult. Before starting, they can tell you which pockets each ball will go into, along with the rails they will use to play position. Normally, most of their shots will follow the original plan; however, it would be unusual if this plan isn't altered a couple of times during the run-out. Only on the routine run-outs do they stick to the original plan precisely. Often when playing 9-ball position, you may get a different angle than you had planned. From this different position, there may be an easier way to play position. It isn't against the rules to change your mind.

Having played a lot of 9-ball, I have noticed three basic shots that pop up rack after rack (Illust. 33, 34, and 35). Although the angles may vary, the fundamental principles are the same. In the illustrations, I have shown what English to use plus the path the cue ball will travel in order to play position on the next ball. On these basic shots, you should be able to play position on a ball anyplace on the table. If other balls are in the way, you must alter the route of the cue ball so that they will be avoided.

Defensive strategy is also an important factor in 9-ball. Sometimes it may be the difference between winning and losing. In Illustrations 36 and 37, I have shown how to leave your opponent a tough shot in case you miss (It is possible). More than likely, you would get another shot if you left your opponent in these two positions. These are just two examples of which there are many, but it should start you thinking. On a low percentage shot, it will be to your advantage to aim the shot so that in case you miss, your opponent will have a tough shot. If you have a high percentage shot, defense should not even cross your mind.

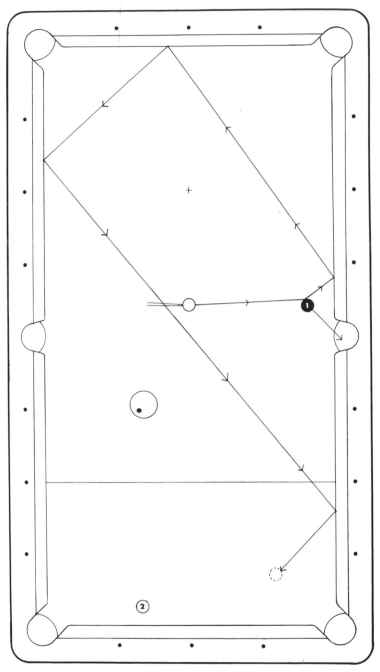

ILLUST. 33 — AROUND THE TABLE FOR POSITION — Use low left
English.

46

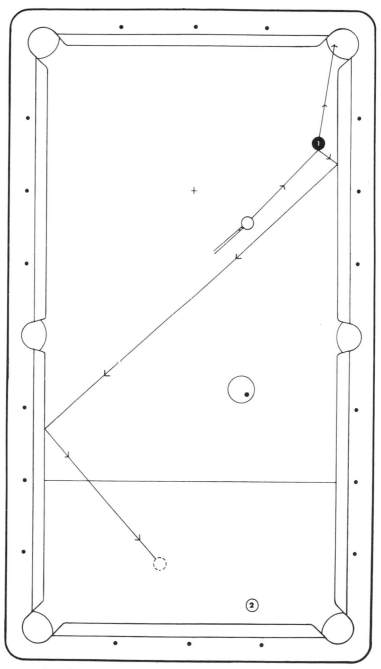

ILLUST. 34 — TWO RAIL POSITION — Use low right English.

47

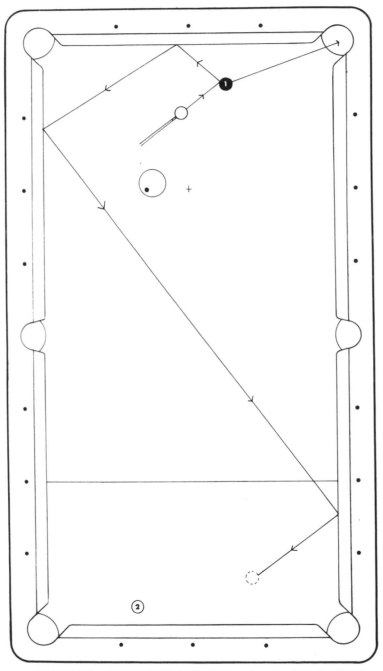

ILLUST. 35 — THREE RAIL POSITION — Use low left English.

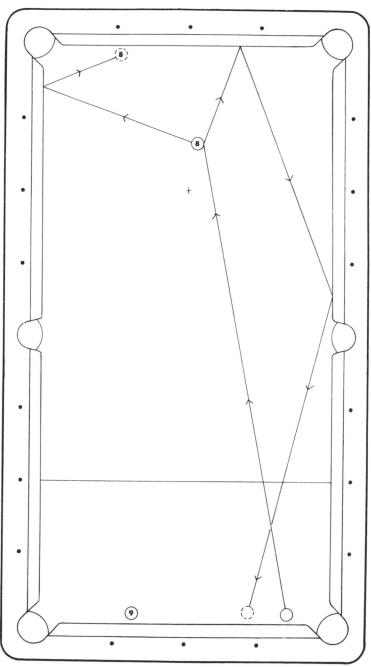

ILLUST. 36 - FREE SHOT - Overcut the shot if you miss so your opponent will have a tough shot left.

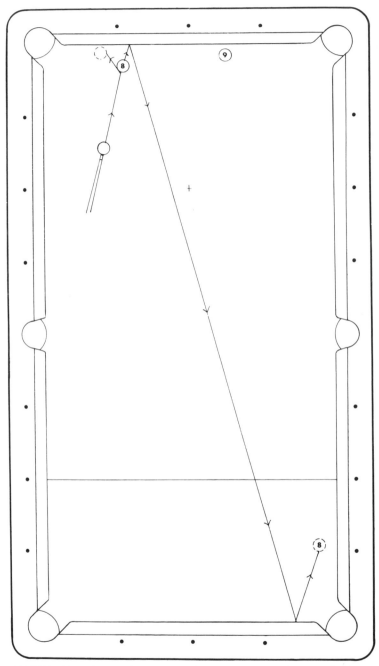

ILLUST. 37 - FREE SHOT - If you miss the bank shot, try to miss it as shown. This way your opponent may make the 8-ball, but he will have difficulty playing position on the 9-ball.

10

PRACTICE DRILLS

Many times I have been asked by students of the game what exercises they can practice to improve their play. Five useful drills are shown in Illustrations 38, 39, 40, 41 and 42.

The first drill in Illustration 38 will teach you speed control. Line up all fifteen balls as shown and try to pocket the balls in order. On the first few tries, you may have trouble finishing the drill. If so, cut down the number of balls to six or eight. Once this becomes too easy, keep adding balls until you can make it using all fifteen. If the drill becomes too easy letting the cue ball bounce off the rails, try the drill **without** letting the cue ball touch a rail. Take my word for it, this will test even the pros. It is not impossible, but close to it!

The next drill (Illust. 39) is a little different. In this drill place the cue ball any place behind the balls that you want. Then try to pocket all fifteen balls in the upper two corner pockets. You can play the balls in any order that you want and in either pocket. Once again, if fifteen balls proves too tough, start with six or eight and work up to the fifteen balls. This drill will help your shot-making ability as well as your position play and this drill is much tougher than the first one. However, if it becomes too easy, try playing them in order from left to right.

The third drill is one that many top players have tried (Illust. 40). The object is to break the balls wide open and try to run as many balls as possible in one of the corner pockets without missing. You begin by trying to break the balls wide open. There are two ways to do this. One is by banking the cue ball off the side rail as shown in the illustration and smacking the right side of the stack. You are trying to spread out as many balls toward the left pocket as possible. The cue ball should end up somewhere to the right of the rack, usually leaving a shot for the left corner pocket. In case of a scratch, you get the cue ball in hand behind the line.

The second method of breaking the balls open is to split the third and fourth balls and scratch in the corner pocket. Hopefully, the rack of balls will spread out toward the left pocket. Since the cue ball is in hand behind the line, you have an excellent chance to have a good shot for the left pocket.

On both break shots, you must shoot hard so as to spread the balls out as much as possible. The break shot is free. But after the break you shoot until you miss, trying to pocket as many balls in the left pocket as you can. Usually the pros try to see how many balls in one pocket they can run with five breaks. In other words, they could get a possible 75. However, 25 to 30 balls in one pocket in five breaks is exceptional. This drill tests both your position play and shot-making.

The fourth drill (Illust. 41) is a frozen ball practice exercise. Most players have trouble making the object ball when it is frozen to the rail. The object of this drill is to make all fifteen balls one at a time without playing any combinations and without the cue ball coming into contact with any of the object balls except the one you are shooting to make. You begin by placing all fifteen balls frozen to the rail as shown in the illustration. Next, you can place the cue ball any place on the table you want in order to begin shooting. But this is the last time you get to place it with your hand. After this you must play position on your next shot. You can play the balls in any order. If fifteen balls prove to be too many, start with a smaller number and work up to fifteen balls. After a few times practicing this drill, your confidence along with your consistency will improve, because you will get used to making the frozen ball by hitting the cue ball with different speeds and with different kinds of English. During this drill, you will get a wide variety of frozen shots and some angles that you may not have seen for some time.

The last drill (Illust. 42) will help you develop consistency on those long straight-in shots. Simply line up the balls across the table from each rail at the diamond as shown and place the cue ball any place behind the line so that you have a straight-in on the first ball. After you make the first ball, again place the cue ball behind the line so that you have a straight-in shot at the next ball. Besides trying to make the ball, experiment making the cue ball stop, draw or follow after you pocket the ball. You can also make the drill tougher by moving the object balls farther away from the cue ball or by moving the cue ball closer to the head rail. Practice this drill a few times and notice the improvement in your ball-pocketing ability.

Often I have been asked, "How long should I practice?" My answer is to practice as long as you are able to concentrate. Once you start to daydream, you might as well quit because you aren't going to accomplish much. I think there is a thin line between **mediocrity** and **excellence** in pool. Perhaps the reason some players cross this line toward excellence is because they are **willing** to **work** a **little harder** than the **others**.

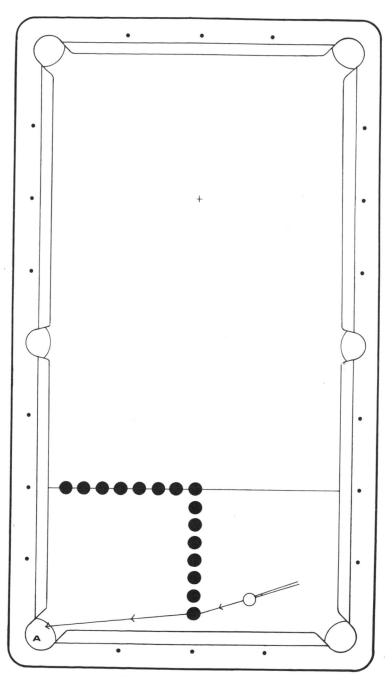

ILLUST. 38 - SPEED CONTROL DRILL

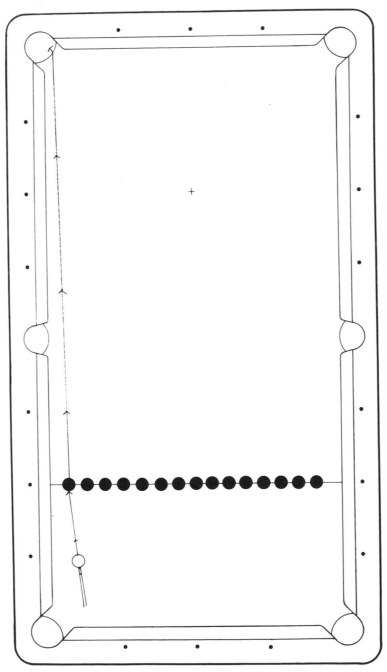

ILLUST. 39 - SHOTMAKING DRILL

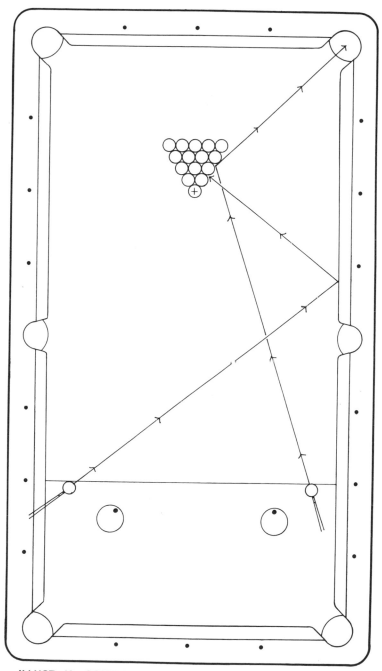

ILLUST. 40 - COMBINATION DRILL - Position play and shotmaking

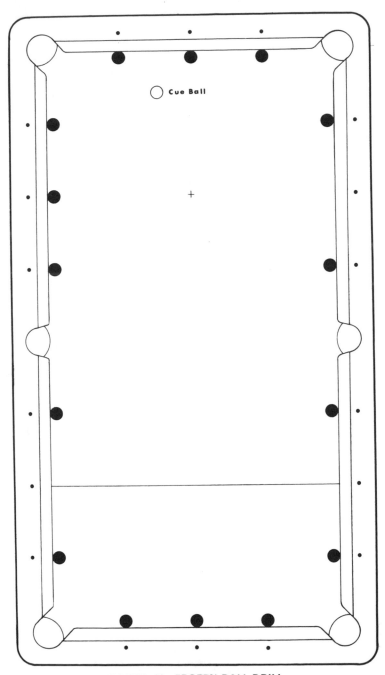

Cue Ball

ILLUST. 41 - FROZEN BALL DRILL

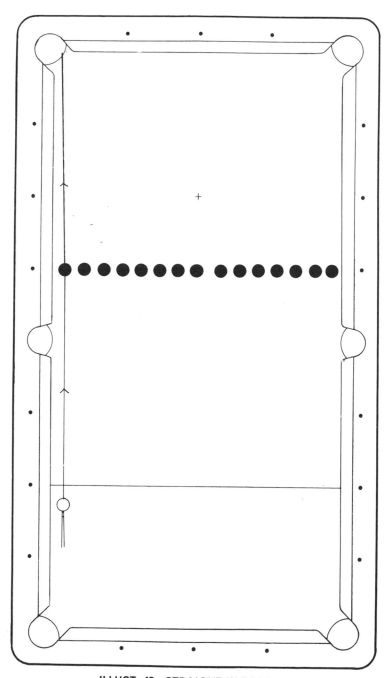

ILLUST. 42 - STRAIGHT-IN DRILL

11

OFFICIAL BCA RULES FOR 8-BALL AND 9-BALL

These rules have been reprinted from the Billiard Congress of America's book titled "The Official Rules and Record Book." I would like to thank the BCA for the permission to use its 8-ball and 9-ball rules in my book. Since the 8-ball and 9-ball rules comprise only six pages out of the 160-page BCA rule book, the inclusion of these rules in this book does not represent a replacement for the BCA rule book. A copy of the BCA rule book should be a "must" for every pool player, and I strongly recommend the purchase of the BCA book.

You can obtain a copy of their book by contacting the BCA at the following address:

Billiard Congress of America
14 S. Linn St.
Iowa City, Iowa 52240
Ph. (319) 351-2112

EIGHT BALL

EIGHT BALL (often called "stripes and solids") is a unique game, and is doubtless the most commonly played pocket billiard game in the U.S. In this game, players must legally pocket seven balls of one group and then legally pocket the eight ball; or pocket the eight ball on a legal break. Recognizing its popularity in facilities utilizing coin-operated tables, the following rules are applicable for commercial, home and coin-operated tables.

PLAYERS: 2 (or 2 teams)

BALLS USED: Standard set of object balls numbered 1-15, plus cue ball; or bi-colored balls (seven each of two colors), plus cue ball and 8-ball.

THE RACK: Standard triangle rack with the apex ball on the foot spot and the 8-ball in the center of the triangle. One ball from each group is put on the two rear corners; other balls may be placed at random.

OBJECT OF THE GAME: To legally pocket all the balls of either group 1-7 (or one color) or 9-15 (or the other color), and then the 8-ball.

SCORING: Group balls have no point value. The player legally pocketing the 8-ball is credited with a game won. (Option: A point system, whereby player winning each game receives three points for winning the game, plus one point for each of opponent's group of balls remaining on the table at game's end.)

OPENING BREAK: Starting player must make an open break or pocket a ball. If he does not make an open break, opponent has the choice of either (1) accepting the table in position and shooting, or (2) having the balls reracked and shooting the opening break shot himself.

DETERMINATION OF GROUPS: Table remains open until a player legally pockets more balls from one group than the other, after an open break; the group from which the greater number of balls was pocketed is then his group.

RULES OF PLAY:

1. A legally pocketed ball of a player's group (a ball of either group when the table is open) entitles shooter to continue at the table until he fails to pocket a ball on a legal shot. After all balls of his group are pocketed, player shoots to pocket the 8-ball.
2. If the 8-ball is pocketed on a legal opening break shot, breaker wins the game. (Option: If the 8-ball is made on the break, the balls are reracked and the breaker breaks the balls again.)
3. Combination shots involving balls of both groups (and/or the 8-ball) are legal when the table is open. After groups are determined, player must cause the cue ball's first contact to be with a ball of his own group. Failure to do so is a foul.
4. When shooting at an open table, player must make the cue ball contact a ball, and then either (1) pocket an object ball, or (2) cause the cue ball or any object ball to contact a cushion. When shooting at his group of balls (or the 8-ball), the cue ball must contact his object ball, and then meet requirements (1) or (2) above. Failure is a foul.

5. When a player has the cue ball in hand behind the head string (as after a scratch), and all his object balls are also behind the head string, the object ball of his group nearest the head string may be spotted on the foot spot at his request (also applies to the 8-ball when it is the object ball). If two or more balls of his group are an equal distance from the head string, the player may also designate which of the equidistant balls he desires to have spotted.
6. When a player has the 8-ball as his object ball and his opponent does not execute a legal shot, player may (1) take shot where cue ball and object balls came to rest, or (2) take cue ball in hand behind the head string, or (3) spot the 8-ball and shoot from within the head string.
7. The 8-ball may not be legally pocketed unless, prior to the shot, the shooting player designates to the opponent (or referee, preferable by physical market) the pocket into which he is playing the 8-ball. (He need designate only the pocket: indicating details such as cushions, banks, kisses, caroms, etc. is not necessary.)

LOSS OF GAME: A player loses the game if he commits any of the following infractions: (a) pockets the 8-ball on an illegal or foul opening break shot; (b) pockets the 8-ball when it is not his legal object ball; (c) pockets the 8-ball on the same stroke as his last group ball(s); (d) scratches when the 8-ball is his legal object ball; (e) jumps the 8-ball off the table at any time during the game; (f) pockets the 8-ball in a pocket other than the one designated; (g) pockets the 8-ball when it is his legal object ball, but without designating the pocket; (h) commits three successive fouls.

ILLEGALLY POCKETED BALLS: Shooter's balls are spotted; opponent's balls remain off the table. Foul penalty 1 applies. (Option: All balls remain off the table.)

JUMPED OBJECT BALLS: Shooter's balls are spotted; opponent's balls remain off the table. No penalty if a legal shot is executed at the same time. (Note the exception of the 8-ball under "Loss of Game" above.)

CUE BALL AFTER JUMP OR SCRATCH: Incoming player has cue ball in hand behind the head string.

PENALTY FOR FOULS: No point penalty. Incoming player has choice of either (1) accepting the table in position and shooting, or shooting with cue ball in hand behind string. However, when the 8-ball is the incoming player's legal object ball, player has choice above, plus choice (3) cue ball in hand behind the head string with the 8-ball spotted on the foot spot.

SPECIAL OPTIONS: Cue ball in hand option: No point penalty. Incoming player has cue ball in hand anywhere on the table. LOSS OF GAME (h) above applied to any third successive foul.

Last pocket option: In this form, the player does not designate into which pocket he will score the 8-ball, but rather is required to pocket the 8-ball into the same pocket that his last group ball was scored. Players must nonetheless confirm the pocket per Rule of Play 6 above.

There are two exceptions to the last pocket requirement: (1) 8-ball pocketed on a legal break shot still wins, regardless of pocket, per Rule of Play 2 above; and (2) scratching when the 8-ball is the object ball is NOT loss of game. (Variation: If agreed, player may designate a legal pocket other than his last group ball's pocket provided that on the shot he causes the cue ball to contact three or more cushions prior to the cue ball contacting the 8-ball and pocketing it. All other rules apply as written above.)

NINE BALL

TYPE OF GAME: Nine ball is a variation of Rotation in which the lowest numbered ball on the table must always be the player's first cue ball contact. If player complies, any pocketed ball counts. For example, if a player strikes the one ball legally, then caroms into the nine ball and causes it to be pocketed, that player wins the game. Nine ball is probably today's most popular action-oriented game, since it is fast, easy for spectators to follow and results in spectacular shot-making; a fast and exciting game.

PLAYERS: 2 or more, though 2, 3, or 4 is generally preferred.

BALLS USED: Object balls 1-9, plus cue ball.

THE RACK: "Diamond" rack (rows of 1-2-3-2-1) with the 1-ball on the foot spot, and the 9-ball in the diamond's center; other balls may be placed entirely at random.

OBJECT OF GAME: To legally pocket the 9-ball.

SCORING: The balls have no point value. The player legally pocketing the 9-ball is credited with a game won.

OPENING BREAK: The starting player must cause the cue ball's first contact to be with the one ball and (1) make an open break, or (2) legally pocket an object ball. If he fails to do so, incoming player has choice of (1) cue ball in hand behind the head string and object balls in position, or (2) having the balls reracked and shooting the opening break shot himself.

RULES OF PLAY:
1. A legal shot requires that the cue ball's first contact be with the lowest numbered ball on the table. A player must then (1) pocket a ball, or (2) cause the cue ball or any object ball to contact a cushion. Failure to meet these requirements is a foul.
2. A legally pocketed ball entitles a shooter to remain at the table until he fails to pocket a ball on a legal shot.
3. When a player legally pockets a ball, he must shoot again. He may not call a safety and spot a pocketed object ball.
4. It is a loss of game if a player commits three successive fouls.

ILLEGALLY POCKETED BALLS: all spotted. (Common option, coin-operated play: None spotted except the game ball.)

JUMPED OBJECT BALLS: All spotted; no penalty if a legal shot is executed at the same time.

CUE BALL AFTER JUMP OR SCRATCH: Incoming player has cue ball in hand.

PENALTY FOR FOULS: The incoming player is awarded cue ball in hand.

OPTIONAL "SHOOT OUT" RULES: The following optional penalties may be used for fouls (with this option, a player may commit an intentional foul to acquire a better position to play an object ball). When a foul is committed the incoming player has the choice of (1) accepting the table in position and shooting, or (2) requiring that the player who fouled shoot again. If the latter option is chosen, and the player commits a second foul, the incoming player is then either awarded cue ball in hand, or may require that the fouling player shoot a third time (Three successive fouls by the same player is an automatic loss of game.)

In "shoot out" rules, the cue ball is put in play behind the head string after a jump or scratch that is not already covered by an award of cue ball in hand. If the lowest numbered object ball is also behind the head string, it is removed from play and the lowest numbered ball outside the headstring becomes the next object ball.

12

WORLD CHAMPIONS

1963 Luther Lassiter
1964 Luther Lassiter
1965 Joe Balsis
1966 Luther Lassiter
1967 Luther Lassiter
1968 Irving Crane
1969 Ed Kelly
1970 Irving Crane
1971 Ray Martin
1972 Irving Crane
1973 Lou Butera
1974 Ray Martin
1975 No Tournament Held
1976 Larry Lisciotti
1977 Alan Hopkins
1978 Ray Martin
1979 Mike Sigel
1980 Nick Varner
1981 Mike Sigel
1982 Steve Mizerak
1983 Steve Mizerak
1984 No Tournament Held
1985 Mike Sigel
1986 Nick Varner

13

TRICK SHOTS

After performing many shows during the last few years, I realize the tremendous popularity of trick shots. What is phenomenal about trick shots is that a person who does not know the difference between an 8-ball and a banana can thoroughly enjoy them. In this book, I have illustrated and explained over 70 incredible trick shots. Now you can reverse the situation; instead of being a spectator, YOU can be the showman.

In most trick shots, one of the real secrets is the set-up. Without proper set-up, you have absolutely no chance. When trying the trick shots, pay particular attention to both the illustration and the explanation. Don't be too surprised if you don't succeed on the first try; however, try to figure out what went wrong and how to correct it. On different equipment (tables, cloth, etc.) the set-up may vary somewhat. I have tried to keep the explanations as simple and brief as possible.

With the aid of this book and a little practice, you should become an instant trick shot wizard. The nice thing about trick shots is that you don't have to be a Champion in order to make them.

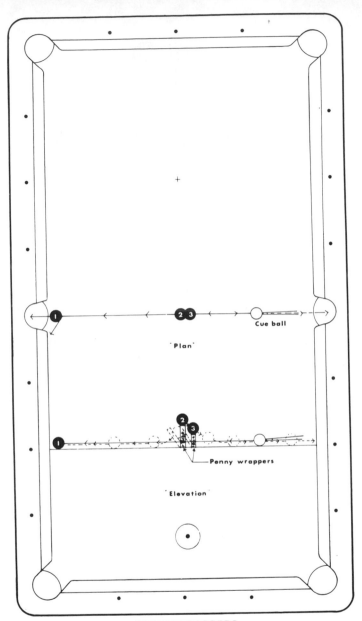

Cue ball

'Plan'

Penny wrappers

'Elevation'

PENNY WRAPPERS

Place the 2-ball and 3-ball on top of the penny wrappers as shown. You will have to cut the penny wrapper that the 3-ball is on so that it is about 2½ inches high. Since the cue ball is 2¼ inches high, you will be able to shoot under the 3-ball without the cue ball touching it. Now put the penny wrappers as close together as you can get them. The 2-ball and 3-ball must be lined up between the two side pockets. Shoot the cue ball into the penny wrappers causing the 2-ball and 3-ball to fall down and kiss. The cue ball will pocket the 1-ball and veer off to the left. Next, the 2-ball will follow into the same pocket as the 1-ball while the 3-ball will go into the right side pocket. Author Robert Byrne showed me the penny wrapper shot at the Caesar's Tahoe 9-Ball Tournament.

66

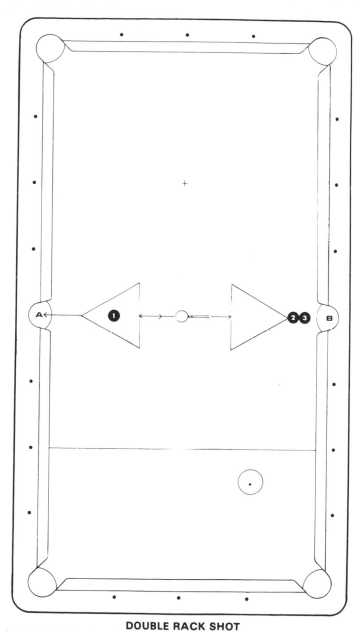

DOUBLE RACK SHOT

EASY, but fun! Simply shoot directly at the triangle with the 1-ball in the center. This will force the triangle toward pocket A, and when the front of the triangle goes over pocket A, it allows the 1-ball to drop into pocket A. The cue ball will bounce back and hit the other rack, pocketing the other two balls in pocket B.

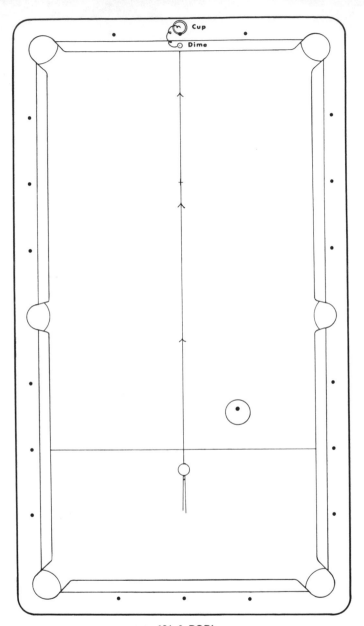

10¢ A POP!

Aim at the dime and hit the cue ball firmly. When the cue ball contacts the cushion, the dime will jump up and into the cup. Placement of the dime and cup plus the proper cue ball speed are very important. With a little practice, you can get this trick down perfect.

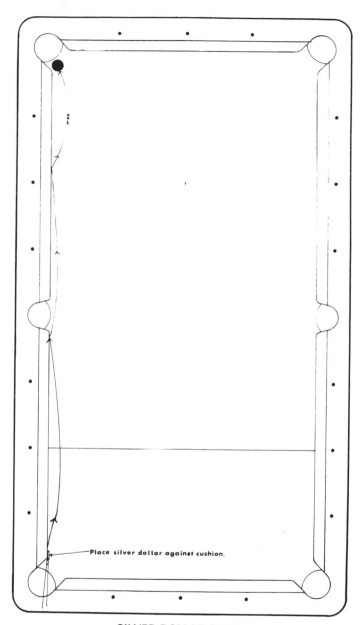

Place silver dollar against cushion.

SILVER DOLLAR SHOT

Place a silver dollar against the rail slanted at a 60 degree angle. Hit the silver dollar in the center. Watch it travel down the table along the path shown to pocket the object ball. Experiment to find the proper speed. Simple shot, but it is a spectator's delight.

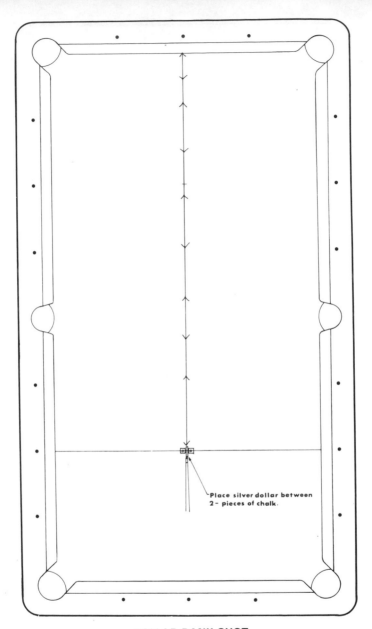

Place silver dollar between 2 - pieces of chalk.

DOLLAR BANK SHOT

Place the silver dollar between two cubes of chalk as shown. You must hit the silver dollar firmly, above the center (so that you don't move the chalk). The silver dollar travels down the table and banks back between the cubes of chalk . . . "Unbelievable!"

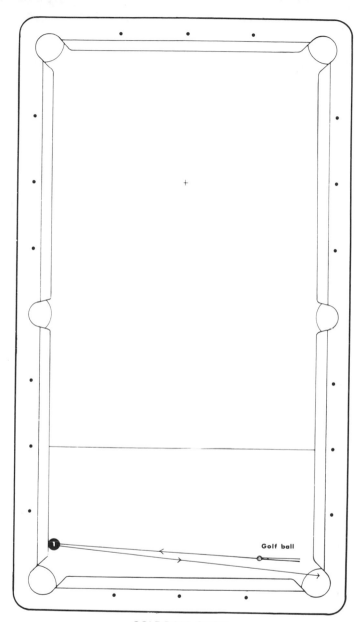

Golf ball

GOLF BALL SHOT

With the cue ball, this shot would be impossible. The 1-ball is frozen against the cushion about 2 inches from the corner pocket. Aim at the 1-ball slightly right of center. Hit the golf ball in the middle. After contact, the 1-ball should bank into the corner pocket.

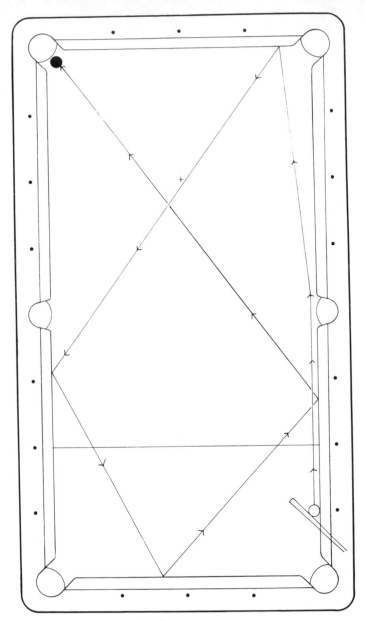

RAKE IT AROUND

One of the first trick shots I learned, simply rake the cue ball with the butt of the cue into the rail, which puts English on the cue ball, sending it five rails to kick in the object ball. I wouldn't use a $300 custom cue for this trick!

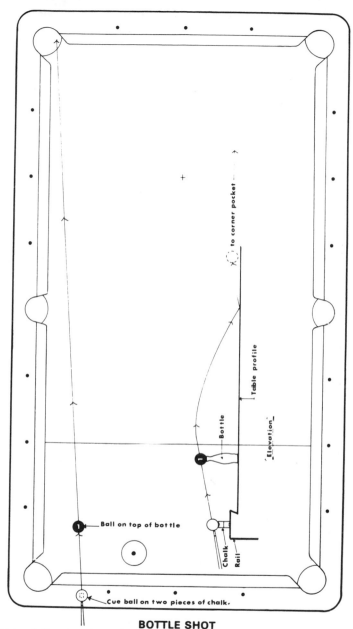

Cue ball on two pieces of chalk.

Ball on top of bottle

to corner pocket

Table profile

Bottle

Elevation

Chalk

Rail

BOTTLE SHOT

Place the cue ball on top of two pieces of chalk as shown in the illustration. The 1-ball is on top of the bottle. Aim at the 1-ball so that you can pocket it in the corner. Practice a few times in order to get the proper speed.

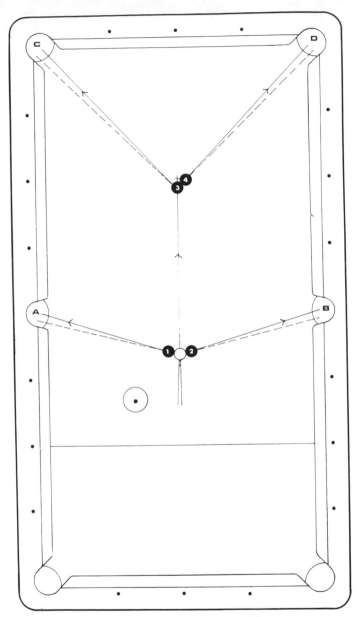

4 TO 4 BY JOHN EDWARDS
Line up the 1-ball, 2-ball, 3-ball and 4-ball along the dotted lines. Aim to hit the 3-ball head on, possible just a fraction right of center. I wanted to name a shot after a friend who showed me how to kill and spin the cue ball.

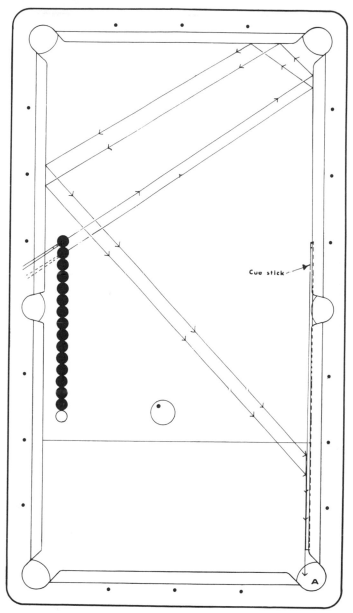

10 SECONDS

Place the cue along the rail as shown. Starting with the first ball, bank all sixteen balls three rails into pocket A. Hit all the balls with high left English. After the first two balls, you have to shoot between two balls as they are coming off the third rail right in front of you. Aim all the balls so that if they miss the pocket they will slide in off the cuestick. Be sure to chalk up. Practice until you can bank all sixteen balls in 10 seconds.

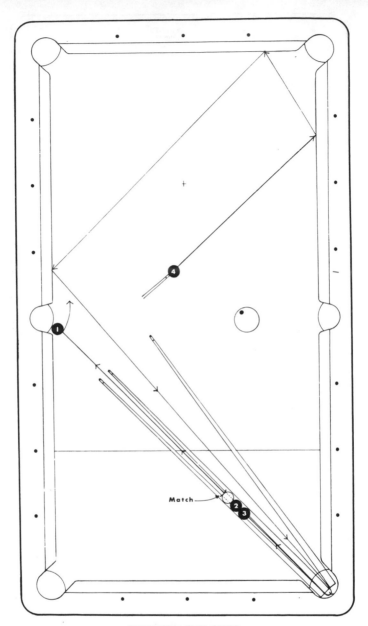

Match

BETWEEN THE CUES

Use a match from a soft matchbook to hold the cue ball, 2-ball and 3-ball in place. Shoot the 4-ball firmly with high left English. The 4-ball goes around the table three rails, between the cues, and then, at the top, comes back down the cues, forcing the other three balls into motion. The cue ball will pocket the 1-ball and glance off to the right while the other three balls follow into the side pocket. You make four balls in rotation.

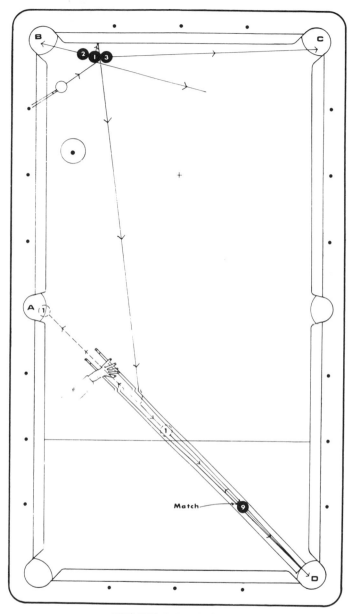

THE GODFATHER SHOT

Paul Lucchesi, a good friend from Massachussetts, showed me this shot. Place the two cues as shown with a soft match holding up the 9-ball. Before you shoot, tell your friends that the 1-ball will go into the side pocket A. This ought to grab them by surprise. Stroke the cue ball firmly and hit the 1-ball just a fraction right of center. As soon as you shoot, place your hand over the two cue sticks as shown. Now watch the 1-ball jump into the track formed by the two cues. Next, the 1-ball will go up the track, kissing the 9-ball into pocket D. The 1-ball will now change direction and follow the track into the side pocket. Caution: the speed of the 1-ball is very important. It must be the proper speed to jump into the track.

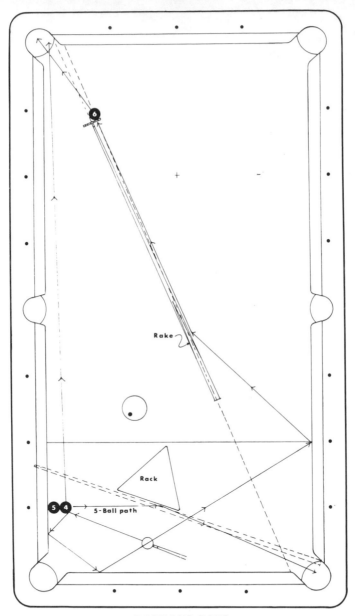

RACK AND RAKE

Set up the 4-ball and 5-ball at the diamond as shown. Now, place your cue on the table as shown in order to get the rack (use wood, not plastic) in the proper place. Now place the rake (bridge) and 6-ball on the table as illustrated. Pick up your cue and aim to hit the 4-ball ⅓ full with low left English, using a firm stroke. Watch the 4-ball travel up the table into the corner pocket. The 5-ball with bank off the rail, hit the rack, and glance into the corner pocket. Meanwhile, the cue ball will travel three rails, hit the rake, and then follow along the rake to contact the head of the rake in order to pocket the 6-ball.

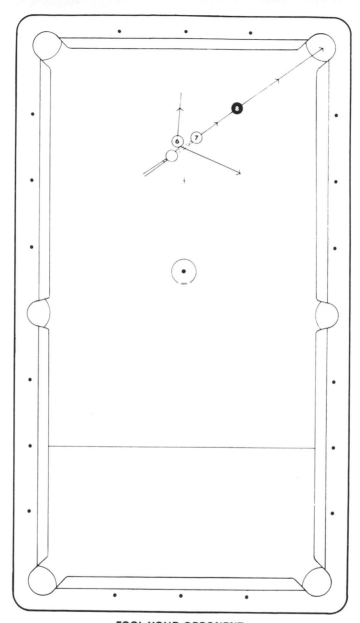

FOOL YOUR OPPONENT

Line up the cue ball, 7-ball and 8-ball on a straight line for the corner pocket. Stroke the cue ball in the center, hard and fast. After the cue ball slides off the 6-ball to the right, continue on with your cue, striking the 7-ball so that it will pocket the 8-ball in the corner. Although this shot is illegal, most people will be fooled. Set it up again. This time shoot slowly and easily so they can see what REALLY happens.

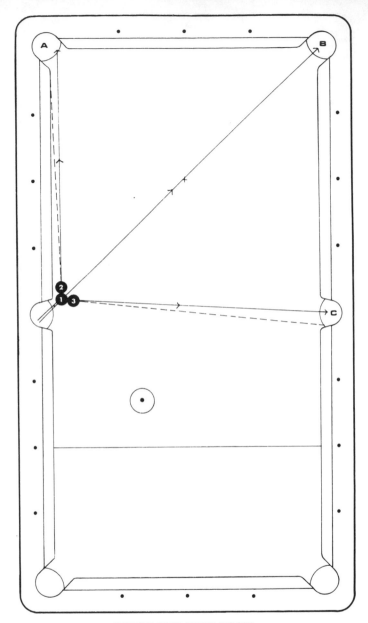

WHICH ONE GOES FIRST?

This is a real beauty. Line up the 2-ball and 3-ball along the dotted lines. Hit the 1-ball **firmly** in the center, and aim at the center of pocket B. (Don't use any side English.)

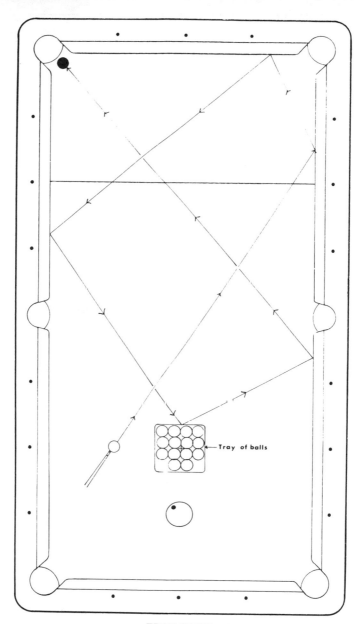

TRAY SHOT

The tray shot is truly unusual. Hit the cue ball firmly with high left English. Aim at the right rail so that the cue ball will come around the table three rails and hit the middle of the tray of balls. The cue ball will bounce off the tray to hit the fourth rail and spin down the table to pocket the object ball.

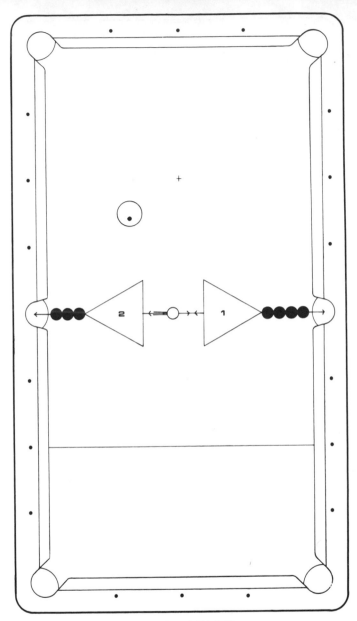

7 BALLS + 2 RACKS

Although it is easy, you will really surprise your audience with this trick. Shoot the cue ball at the triangle with four balls. The cue ball will then bounce back, hitting the second triangle. Both triangles will force all the balls into the side pockets. 7 balls - 1 shot ... not bad, eh!

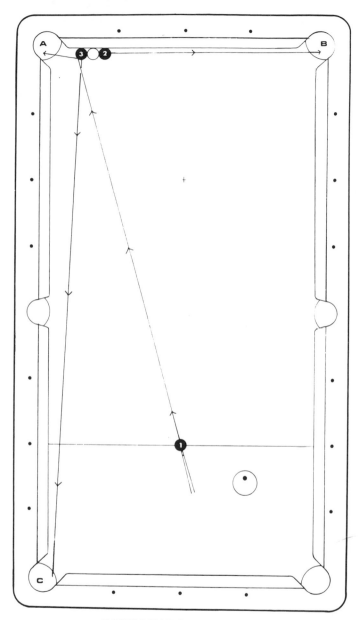

DON'T MOVE THE CUE BALL

Carefully study the position of the balls because set-up is most important. Aim the 1-ball to kiss off the 3-ball into pocket A. The 2-ball will go into pocket B, and the 3-ball into pocket C, while the cue ball will remain in the same position.

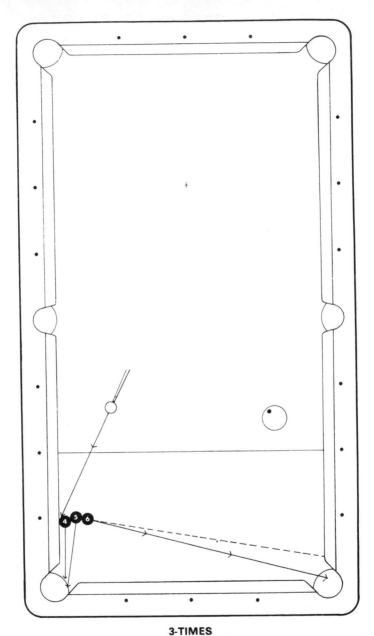

3-TIMES

Line up the 5-ball and 6-ball along the dotted line. Aim to make the 4-ball with high left English. The 4-ball and 5-ball will go in the left corner pocket and the 6-ball travels across the table into the right pocket.

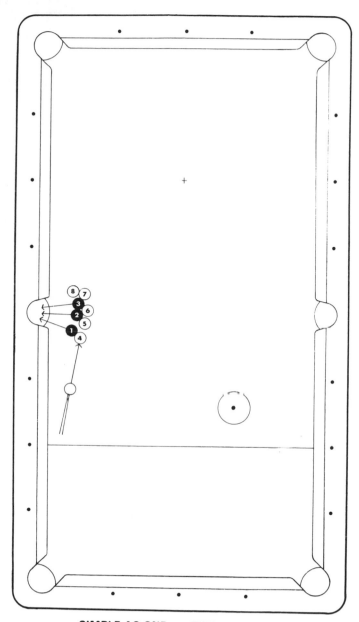

SIMPLE AS ONE ... TWO ... THREE

A former National Collegiate Champion (the only three-time winner) and a good friend of mine, Leroy Kinman, showed me this great shot. It is set up to pocket the 1-ball, 2-ball and 3-ball in rotation. Proper set-up is a necessity. In particular, be sure the 2-ball kisses off the 3-ball, and the 5-ball hits the 6-ball, which causes the 3-ball to kiss off the 7-ball and 8-ball. Aim at the center of the 4-ball.

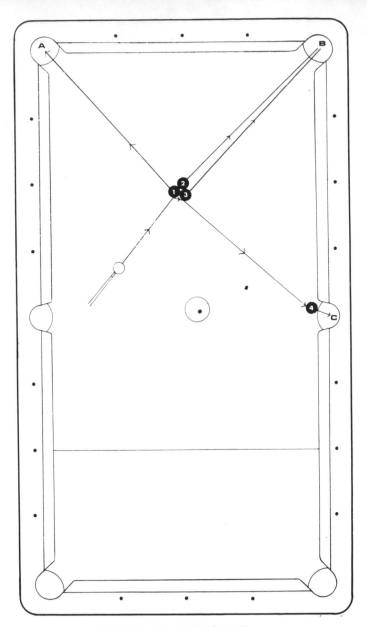

FOUR INTO THREE EQUALS . . .

On this shot, the 2-ball is **on the spot.** Aim at the 1-ball a little right of center. The cue ball will slide off the 1-ball, kiss the 3-ball into the corner pocket and slide off the 3-ball to kiss the 4-ball in.

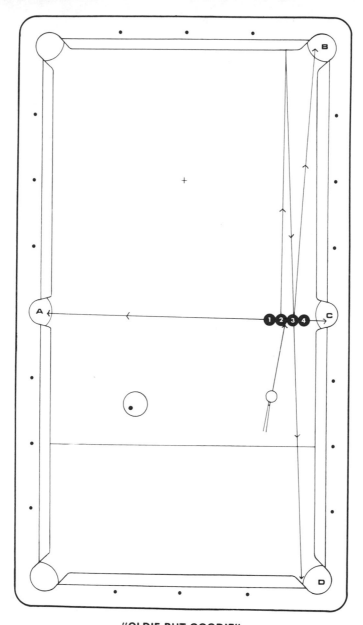

"OLDIE BUT GOODIE"

Try to hit the 2-ball just a fraction before the 3-ball. The 2-ball banks back into pocket D. Be sure to hit the cue ball with low left English.

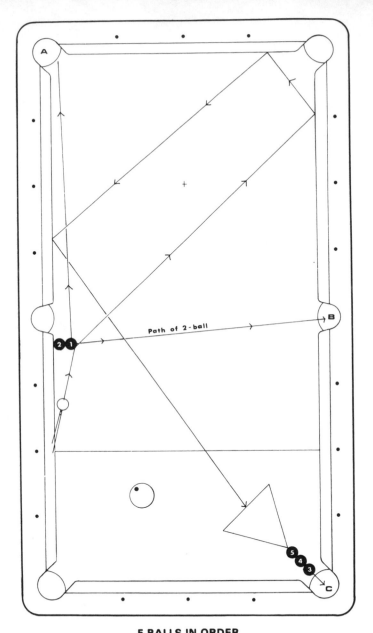

Path of 2-ball

5 BALLS IN ORDER

For you bank lovers, aim to hit the 1-ball on the right side, almost ⅓ or ¼ full. Watch the cue ball circle the table and hit the rack, pocketing the other three balls.

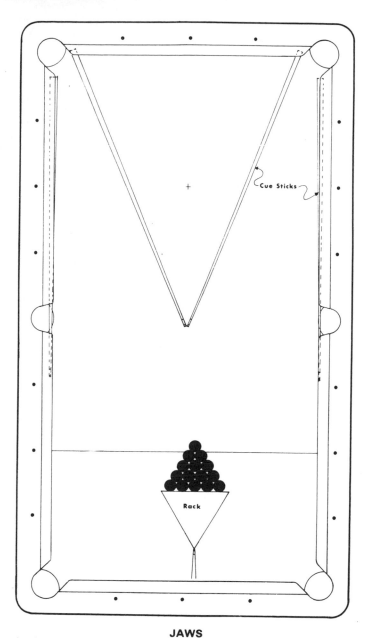

Cue Sticks

Rack

JAWS

Line up the shot above as shown. Place the tip of your cue against the rack and push through firmly. Experiment to find the proper speed. Once the balls start rolling the cue sticks will guide all fifteen balls into the upper two corner pockets.

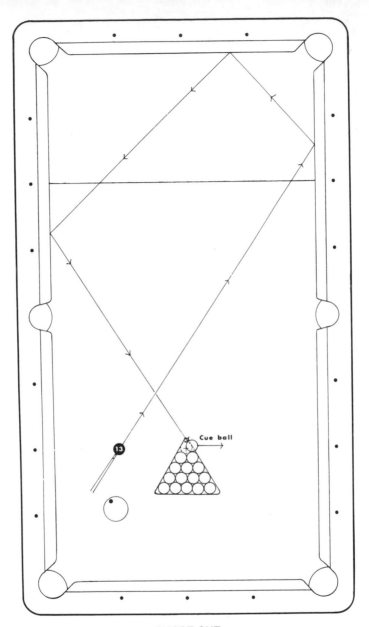

Cue ball

SHORT CUT

Rack up the balls and then prop up the rack on top of the cue ball. On most tables, aim the 13-ball at the first diamond with high left English. The 13-ball will travel around the table three rails and go under the rack to knock the cue ball out. Now, the 13-ball will end up at the front of the rack and the rack will drop down. Not a bad way to rack the balls!

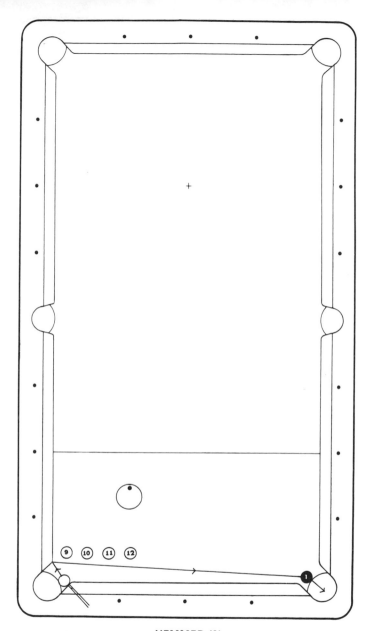

HEMMED IN

Shoot the cue ball into the point of the corner pocket. The cue ball will bank off the point while missing the balls and travel along the end rail to pocket the 1-ball.

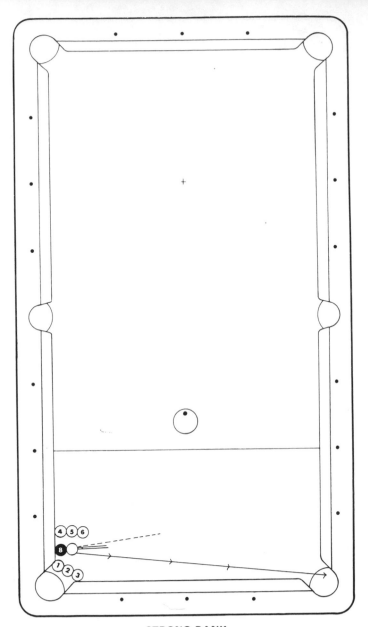

STRONG BANK

Elevate your cue about 30 degrees. Hit the cue ball firmly and above the center. When your tip contacts the cue ball, let it slide right over the top of the cue ball so that your cue won't interfere with the shot. The 8-ball should bank across the table into the corner pocket without the cue ball or the 8-ball touching any of the surrounding six balls.

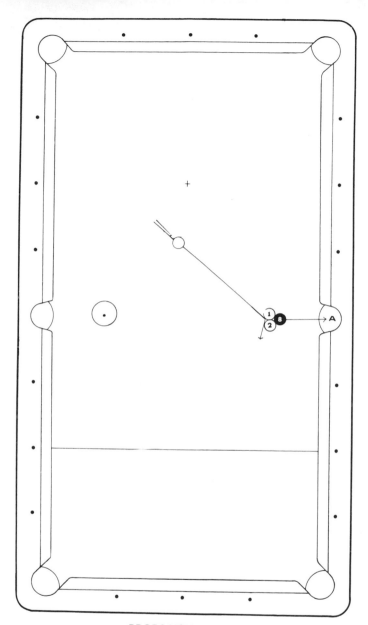

PROPOSITION SHOT

On this trick shot, you must place the cue ball as shown instead of putting it between the side pockets as most people would do. Now, aim to hit the 1-ball **really** thin and watch the black ball disappear into the side pocket.

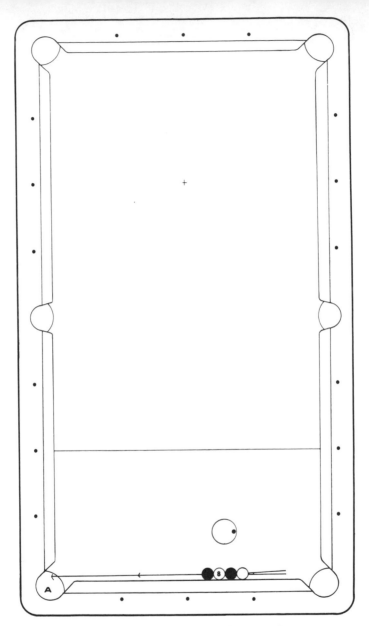

TAKE THIS SHOT AND "SHOVE" IT

Aim straight ahead at the three object balls using right English. However, **PUSH** the cue ball forward, don't shoot it as you normally would. Then, watch the two black balls go into pocket A without making the 8-ball.

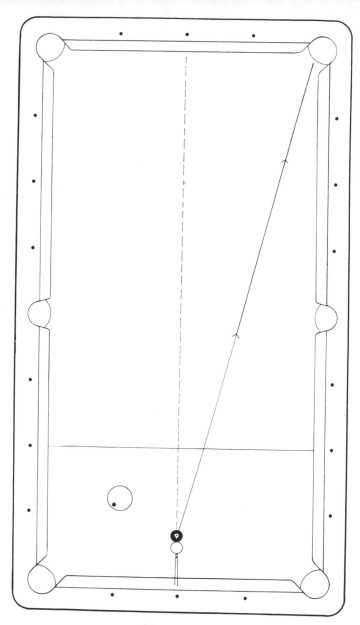

CHALK BALLS

Put some chalk (from a regular stick of chalk) on the contact point of both the cue ball and 9-ball. Hit the cue ball with low left English. It might help throw the 9-ball more if you aim toward the right corner pocket. Watch the 9-ball disappear into the corner pocket.

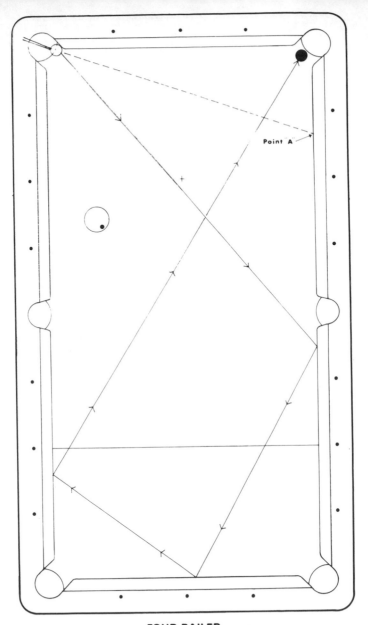

Point A

FOUR RAILER
The cue ball is frozen against the point of the corner pocket. Aim the cue ball at point A using low right English with a firm stroke. Then watch the cue ball travel around the table to pocket the black ball.

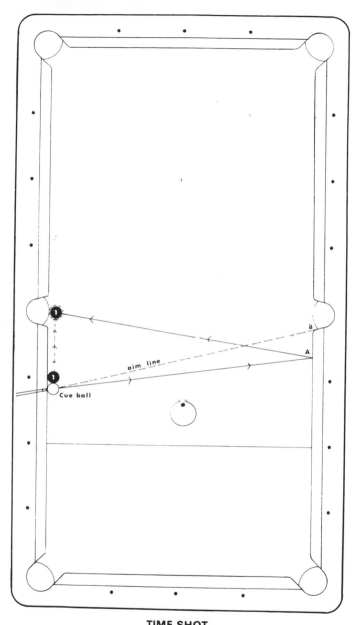

TIME SHOT

Aim the cue ball across the table at point B. If your timing is good, the cue ball will bank off the rail (at point A) and kiss the 1-ball into the side pocket.

CARD SHOT

Each of the seven balls is resting on the top of a rolled-up playing card. Aim at the 8-ball and hit the cue ball firmly. Watch the cue ball going under all the balls, scattering the cards and pocketing the 8-ball. You will create some enthusiasm with this shot.

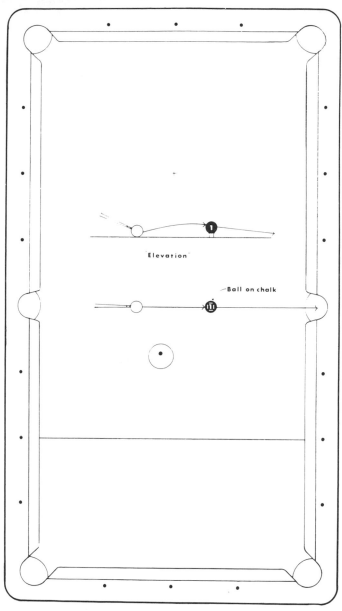

Elevation

Ball on chalk

CHALK IT UP

Place the 1-ball on a piece of chalk as shown in the illustration. Elevate the cue about 45 degrees and contact the cue ball above the center firmly. Aim dead center at the 1-ball. Then watch it sink into the side pocket.

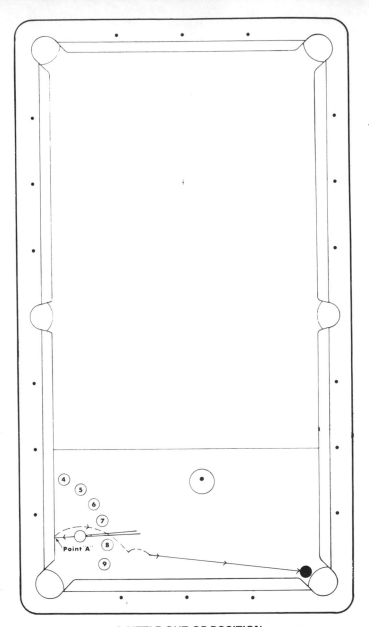

A LITTLE OUT OF POSITION

If you drive a car, you know that the shortest route is not always the fastest or best. During a game, should you find yourself in this position, just change direction. Since you can't go forward, just go the other way. Elevate your cue about 45 degrees and hit the cue ball firmly and above the center, aiming at point A. After hitting the rail, the cue ball will jump over the balls and pocket the object ball.

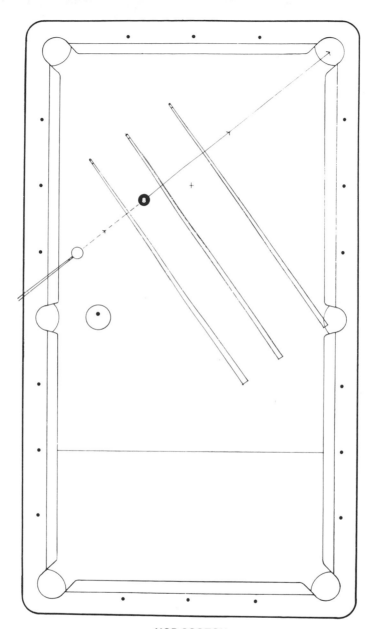

HOP SCOTCH

On this shot, elevate your cue about 45 degrees. Elevating your cue causes you to shoot down into the cue ball. This, in turn, makes the cue ball jump over the cue. Next the cue ball will contact the 8-ball, making it jump over the other two cues and into the corner pocket. Hit the cue ball above center with a firm stroke.

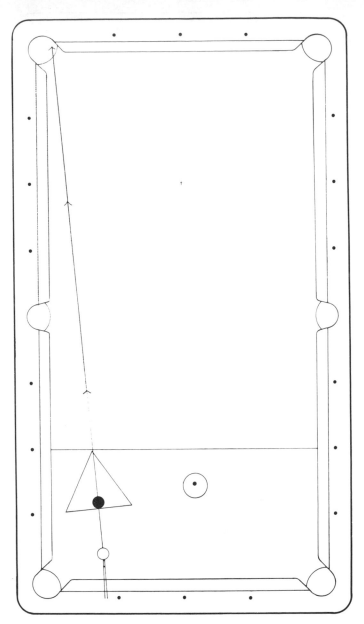

AN OLD FAVORITE

One of my favorite shots, even though it doesn't come up too often in a game, begins by elevating the cue about 45 degrees. Hit the cue ball above the center with a firm stroke. The cue ball will cause the object ball to jump out of the triangle and go into the corner pocket. You'll feel like an old pro!

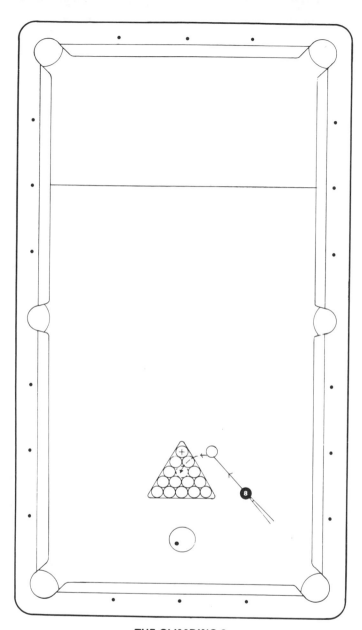

THE CLIMBING 8

When playing 8-ball, everyone knows that the 8-ball is supposed to go in the center of the rack. Here is an eye-catching way to put it there. Elevate the cue about 45 degrees; hit the 8-ball firmly and aim the 8-ball so that it will contact the cue ball slightly left of center. After hitting the cue ball, the 8-ball will jump to the left and above the rack. Then, the 8-ball will drop into the center of the rack - a jump and billiard shot.

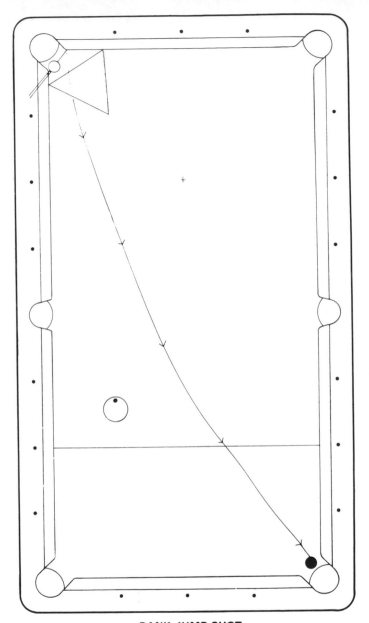

BANK JUMP SHOT

I found this trick shot by accident while practicing one day. Elevate the cue about 45 degrees and hit the cue ball firmly. Shoot into the point of the corner pocket. The cue ball should bank off the point, climb over the rack, and travel down the table to pocket the object ball.

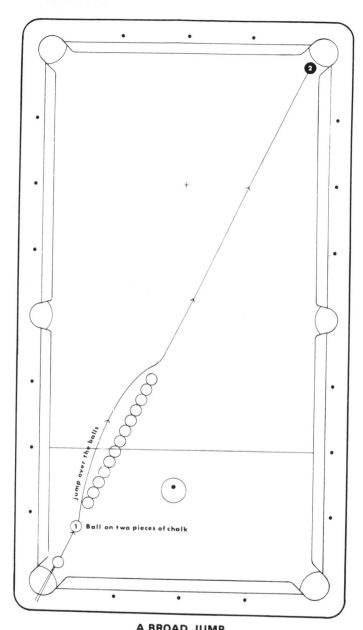

jump over the balls

① Ball on two pieces of chalk

A BROAD JUMP

Place the 1-ball on the top of two chalk cubes. Elevate the cue about 45 degrees and contact the cue ball above the center, **stroking firmly.** Aim dead center at the 1-ball. It will jump over the 13 balls and travel down the table to pocket the 2-ball. Quite a jump shot!

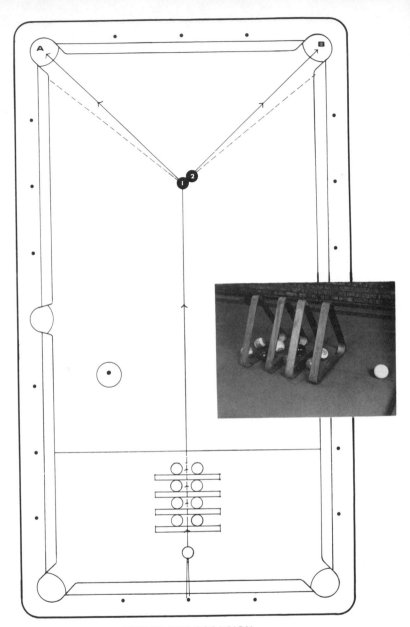

RISE TO THE OCCASION

On this shot, the balls are close enough together that the cue ball cannot go between them. Place the triangles upright as shown in the illustration. Line up the 1-ball and the 2-ball along the dotted lines. Elevate the cue about 45 degrees, stroke the cue ball firmly and slightly above the center. The cue ball will jump over the balls and the triangles, and travel down the table to pocket the 1 and 2-balls. Hit the 1-ball dead center.

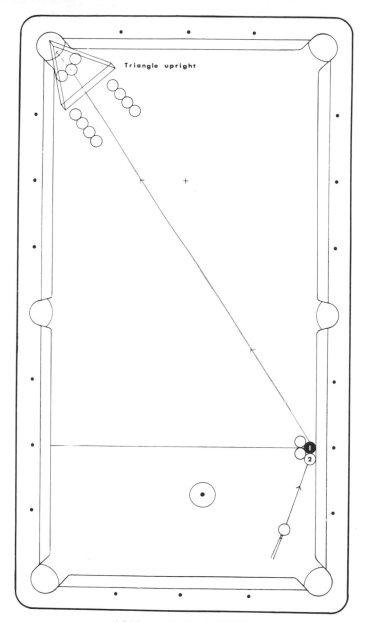

Triangle upright

LEAP INTO THE CORNER

Place triangle against both rails. Aim head on at the 2-ball stroking the cue ball firmly and in the center. The 1-ball will bank off the cushion, go through the two rows of balls, hit the rack and hop over the three balls into the corner pocket. This shot is a real "attention-getter." Proper speed is very important along with the placement of the 1-ball. You may have to move it along the rail until the proper place is found.

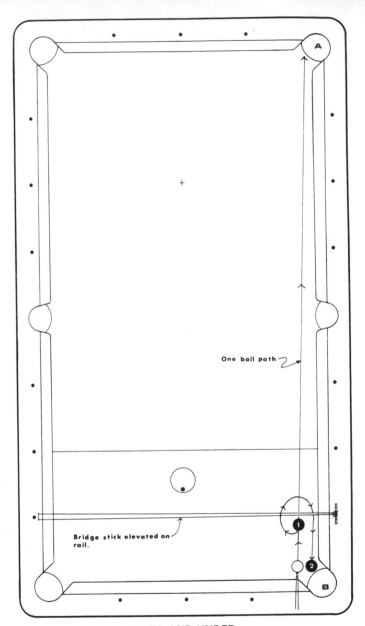

One ball path

Bridge stick elevated on rail.

OVER AND UNDER

Now, try a real skill shot. Elevate your cue about 45 degrees, and contact the cue ball below the center. Aim head on at the 1-ball, sending it into pocket A. After contacting the 1-ball, the cue ball will jump over the bridge stick, land on the table, and then draw back under the bridge stick to pocket the 2-ball. Shoot hard. This shot has been known to "bring the house down!"

PYRAMID SHOT
Set up balls as shown. Aim at the ball on top in order to pocket it in the corner. Use two pieces of chalk to hold the ball on top.

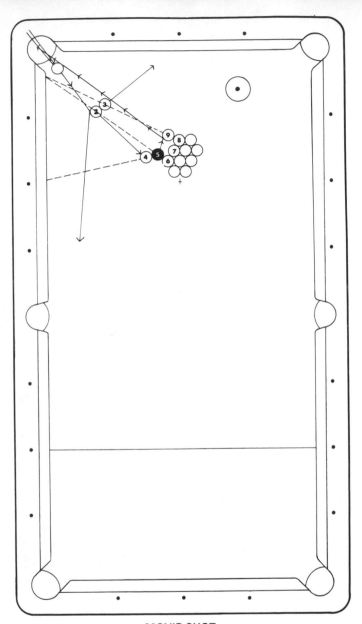

MOVIE SHOT

Start with the balls racked up. Line up the following balls along the dotted lines: 4-ball and 5-ball, 5-ball and 6-ball, 8-ball and 9-ball. Aim to hit the 2-ball just a fraction right of center with a firm stroke. The 2-ball and 3-ball are lined so that when the cue ball hits the 2-ball it will kiss the 3-ball out of the way. Next, the 2-ball travels ahead to hit the 4-ball, which will drive the 5-ball into the 6-ball, 7-ball and 9-ball on its way to the corner pocket. On this shot as on about all mystery ball shots, proper set-up is a necessity. With proper set-up, the mystery ball shots are almost impossible to miss.

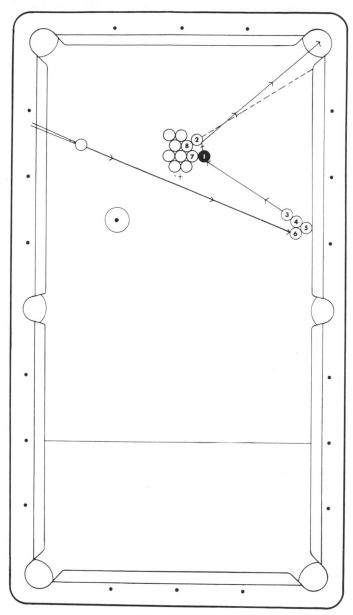

THE HARD WAY

Begin by racking up the balls. Remove the four balls (3-ball, 4-ball, 5-ball and 6-ball) from the rack and place them along the rail as shown. The 3-ball must be lined up to hit the 1-ball left of center so that the 1-ball will kiss off the 7-ball and go down to kiss off the 2-ball into the corner pocket. Line up the 8-ball and 2-ball along the dotted line. Aim to hit the 6-ball firm and head on.

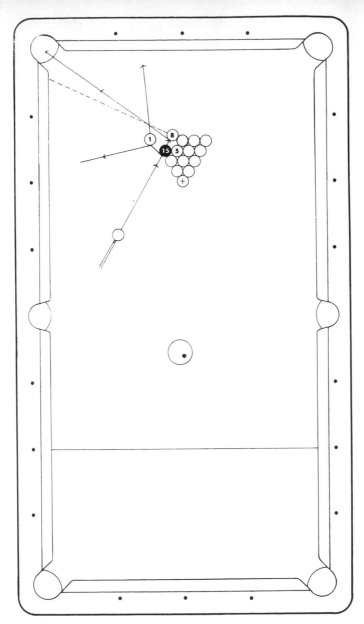

STACK SHOT

Rack up all fifteen balls. Begin by moving the corner ball (1-ball) 1 to 1½ inches to the left. Next move the 8-ball so that it is lined up along the dotted line. Aim left of center at the black ball so that the cue ball will slide over to push the 1-ball out of the way. Hit the cue ball firmly with low right English. Watch the black ball kiss off the 5-ball and 8-ball as it travels to the corner pocket.

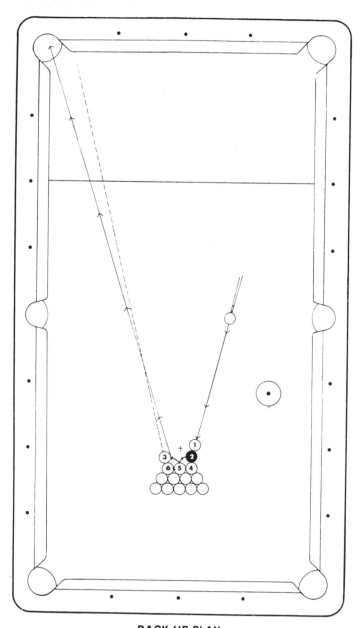

BACK UP PLAY

Hit the 1-ball head on with a firm stroke. The 2-ball will kiss off the 4-ball, 5-ball and 3-ball and travel up the table to fall into the corner pocket. The 3-ball and 6-ball are lined up along the dotted line.

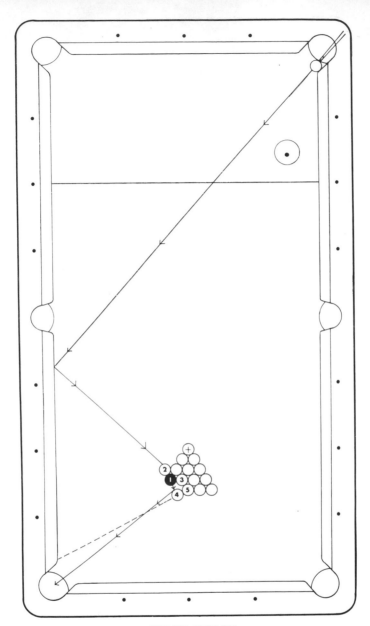

SNEAK ATTACK

Aim at the diamond below the side pocket and contact the cue ball below the center. The cue ball will bank off the rail into the 2-ball, which will cause the 1-ball to kiss off the 3-ball and 4-ball into the corner pocket. Notice the 4-ball and 5-ball are lined up along the dotted lines.

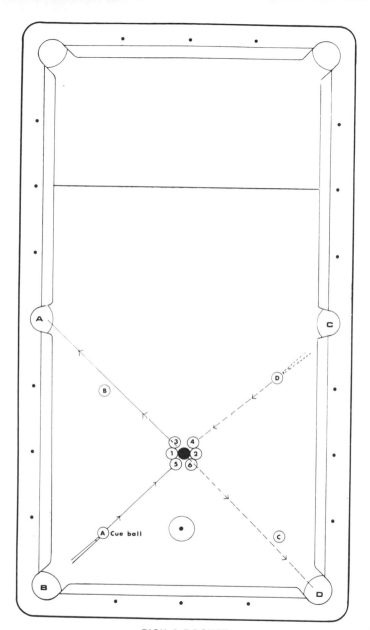

PICK A POCKET

Place the black ball on the spot. The 3, 4, 5, and 6-balls should all be about ½ inch from the black ball. (This is the real secret of the shot.) On different tables, this distance may vary either closer or farther. You can pocket the black ball in any of the four pockets (A, B, C, OR D). The pocket which is chosen determines the position of the cue ball. If pocket A is selected, place the cue ball in the A position. Hit the cue ball firmly in the center. Aim head on at the 5-ball. Watch the black ball disappear into the side pocket.

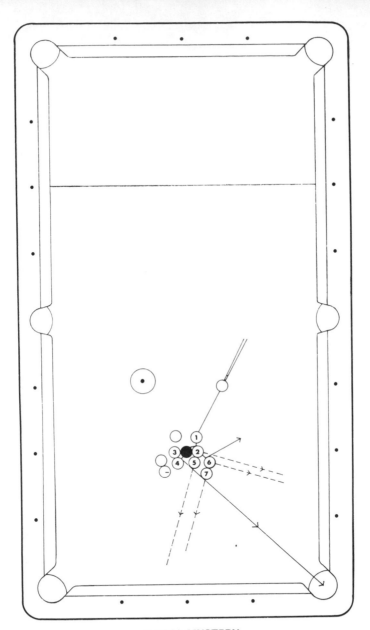

A REAL MYSTERY

Place the black ball on the spot. The real secrets to this shot are proper set-up and the placement of the 4-ball. Normally, the 4-ball should be about ½ inch from the black-ball. Aim at the 1-ball so that it will hit the 2-ball slightly before it hits the black ball. The 2-ball clears balls 5, 6, and 7 out of the way so that the black ball will kiss off the 3-ball and 4-ball into the corner pocket. If the black ball hits the end rail instead of pocket, place the 4-ball a little closer to the black ball.

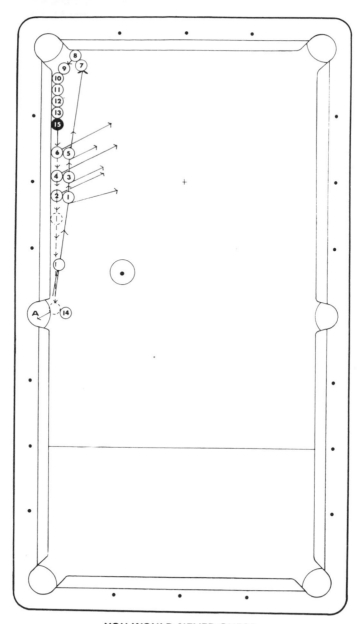

YOU WOULD NEVER GUESS

Set up the balls as shown. Aim to hit the 1-ball slightly right of center. Stroke the cue ball firmly and below the center. The 1-ball will hit the 3-ball, which will hit the 5-ball. This causes the 2-ball, 4-ball, and 6-ball to move out of the way. The 5-ball continues down to hit the 7-ball, which drives the 8-ball off the cushion. The 8-ball will hit the 9-ball, causing the 15-ball to move along the rail toward the side pocket where it kisses off the 14-ball.

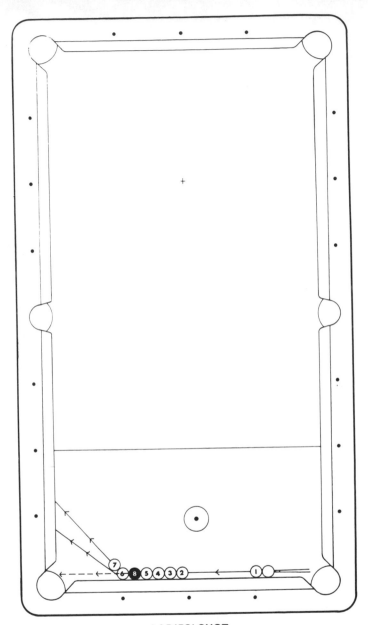

LADIES' SHOT

Aim straight ahead at the row of balls and hit the cue ball firmly and in the center. Watch the 6-ball and 7-ball clear out of the way. Then the 8-ball will follow right into the corner pocket.

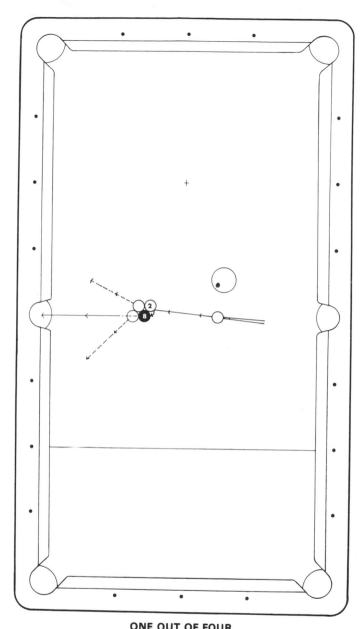

ONE OUT OF FOUR

Aim left of center at the 2-ball. The 2-ball will clear the other two object balls out of the 8-ball's path. Then, the cue ball will slide off the 2-ball, contacting the 8-ball so that the 8-ball will go into the side pocket.

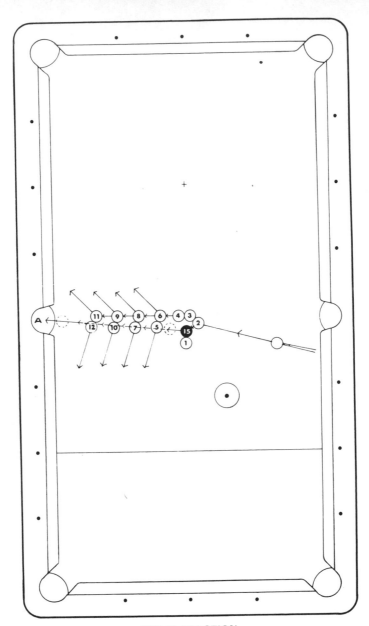

CHAIN REACTION

Set up the balls as shown. Hit the 2-ball head on. Stroke the cue ball firmly and a little below center. The 4-ball will split the eight balls so that when the 2-ball hits the black ball, it has a clear path to the side pocket. Proper set-up is a necessity on this shot.

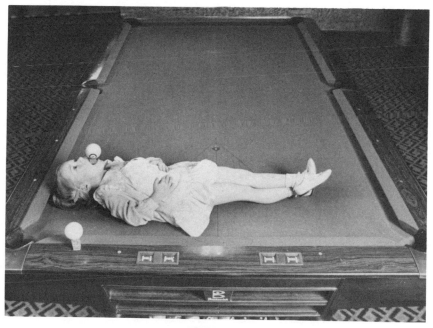

APRIL JILL

My daughter was not crazy about posing for this shot. Get a volunteer to lie down on the table. Next, have the person hold a piece of chalk with his teeth. Put a ball on top of the chalk. Place the cue ball on top of two pieces of chalk as shown. Now, just pick out the spot on the ball that you must hit in order to pocket it in the corner. On this shot, I hope you hit the cue ball at the proper speed.

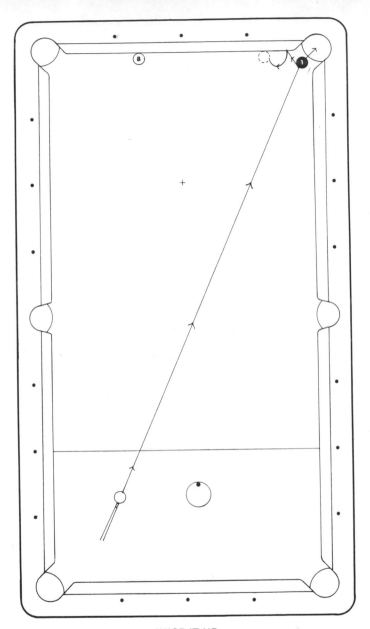

JUICE IT UP

Your friends will get a real kick out of this one. Tell them that you have found a great way to play position on the 8-ball. Aim slightly left of center (almost head on) at the 1-ball. Hit the cue ball hard with high English. Watch the cue ball come off the rail and grab. It may even go back into the rail again. Anyway, you will be left with an easy shot on the 8-ball while amazing your friends.

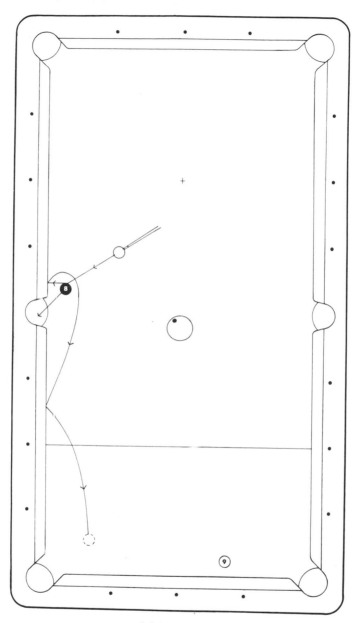

9-BALL SHOT

Line up the 8-ball and the cue ball so that to make the 8-ball, you have to hit the 8-ball slightly right of center. The 8-ball must not be very far from the pocket (3 or 4 inches). Hit the cue ball firmly and with high left English. The cue ball will go into the rail, bounce off, and then loop down the table, leaving you with an easy shot on the 9-ball. If you are looking for a game, try to save this shot for later!

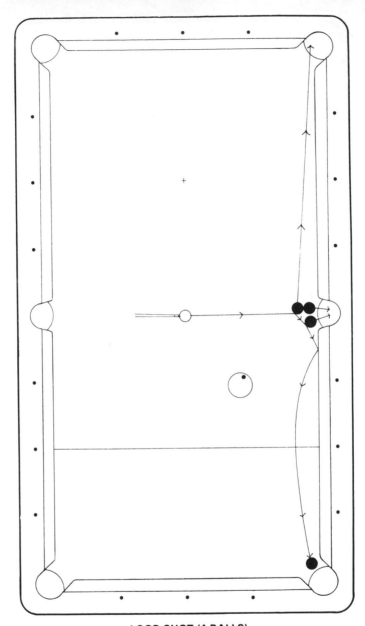

LOOP SHOT (4 BALLS)

Hit the cue ball firmly with high right English. Aim to hit the front ball as shown just a fraction right of center. Then watch the balls disappear!

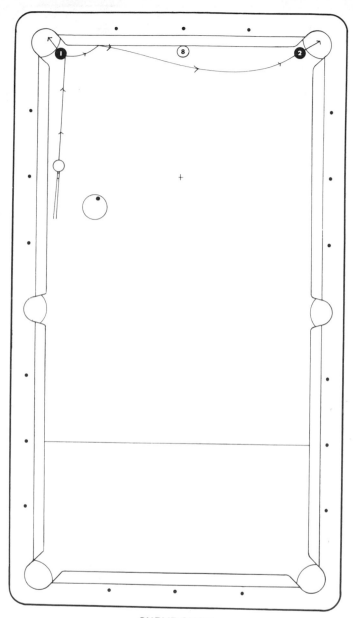

CURVE SHOT

On this shot the ball in the middle blocks your path, which forces you to curve around it. Aim slightly right of center at the 1-ball. Stroke the cue ball firmly with high right English. The cue ball will slide off the 1-ball, bounce off the rail and curve around the middle ball to pocket the 2-ball.

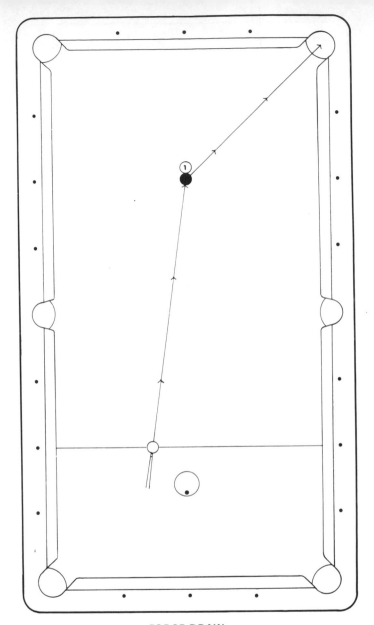

FORCE DRAW
This shot comes up in many games and is very difficult. Place the cue ball left of the spot a few inches. Aim head on at the front ball and hit the cue ball with low draw English. If you hit it good, the front ball should go into the corner pocket. Don't hit the front ball too far left.

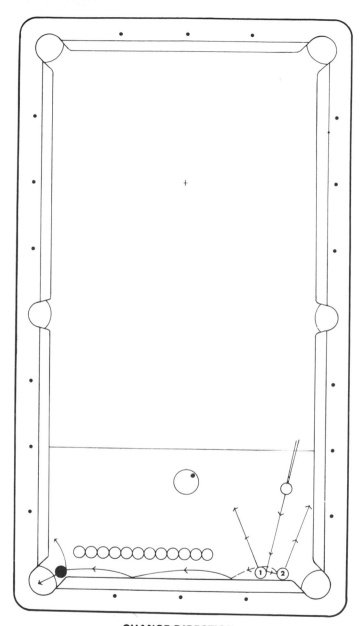

CHANGE DIRECTION

Aim a fraction left of center on the 1-ball (so that the cue ball and 1-ball won't double kiss). Hit the cue ball firmly with high right English. The cue ball will glance off the 1-ball to contact the 2-ball. After touching the 2-ball the cue ball will go the other direction. As it travels along the rail toward the black object ball, it will scatter the object balls. The final result . . . pocketing the black object ball.

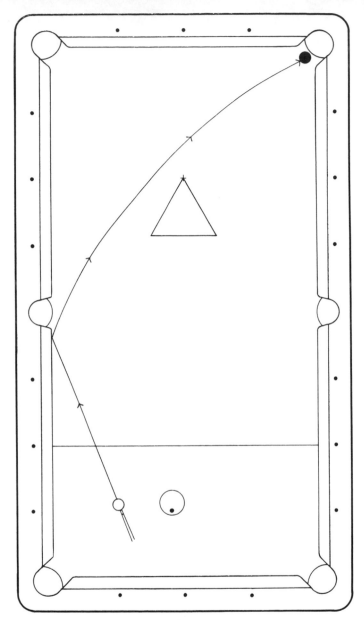

DRAW AROUND RACK

Aim the cue ball close to the point of the side pocket as shown. Hit the cue ball with low draw English and watch it curve around the rack to pocket the object ball.

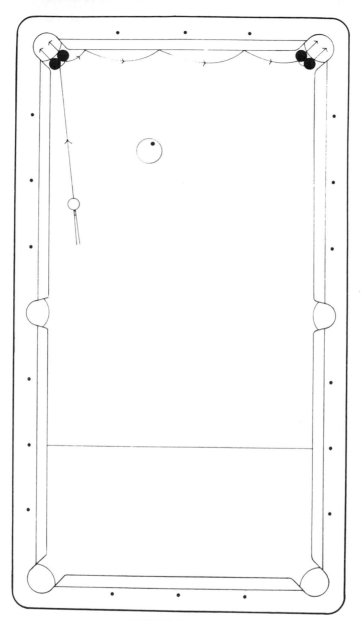

DOUBLE TROUBLE

Hit the cue ball with high right English using a firm stroke. Aim to hit the left black ball a little before the second black ball. You will pocket these two balls in the left pocket. Then the cue ball will loop along the rail pocketing the other two balls in the right pocket.

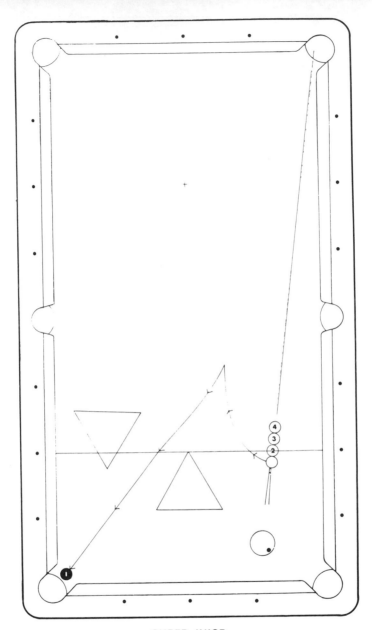

SUPER JUICE

Spectators love this one because it is a real stroke tester. Aim straight ahead at the three balls, stroking the cue ball very firmly with low right English. The cue ball should go forward above the triangles and then, when the low English takes effect, draw back between the two triangles to pocket the 1-ball as shown. You may need 3 or 4 tries on this one.

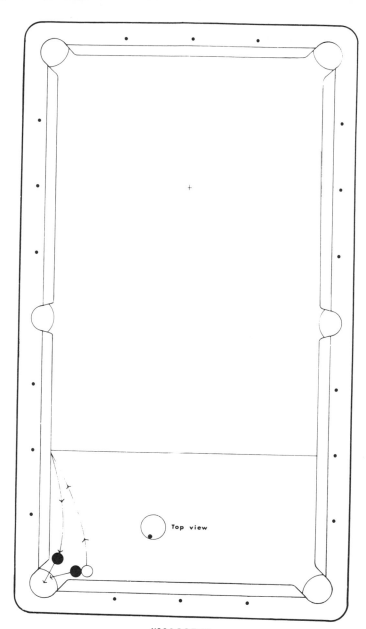

Top view

"MASSEY"

Not only can this shot be dangerous for your bedcloth but also for your cue. Elevate the cue so that it is almost straight up in the air. Strike the cue ball firmly as shown. The cue ball will force the first object ball in, slide forward, and then draw back to pocket the second ball. I prefer to borrow a cue for this trick. After trying it, you will agree with me! The trick above is named after a friend of mine. Mike Massey, because he hits it so great.

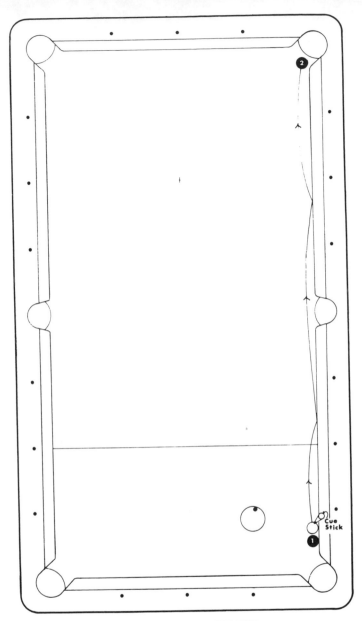

Cue
Stick

MILLION DOLLAR STROKE

Like all masse' shots, this one is sensational, but most room owners do not appreciate it. Your cue stick will be almost vertical. Hit the edge of the cue ball. The cue ball will pocket the 1-ball. Next, the extreme English will grab and cause the cue ball to travel along the rail at a very fast speed to pocket the 2-ball. Caution: one time my shaft shattered into many pieces when I tried this trick. It happened when I was putting on a show at Case Western Reserve University in Cleveland. Maybe you will have better luck!

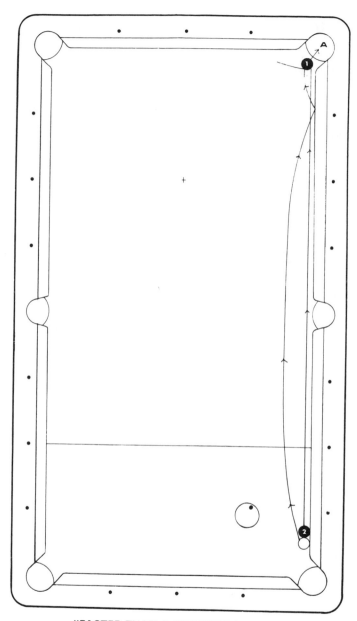

"FASTER THAN A SPEEDING BULLET"

If I had a chapter in my book entitled "Don't try these shots," the trick shot above would definitely be in that chapter. It is extremely difficult. Begin by elevating your cue about 60 degrees and aim to hit the cue ball almost on top with right English. You must aim at the 1-ball and hit the cue ball firmly. As the cue ball and 2-ball travel down the table, the cue ball will go around the 2-ball and pocket the 1-ball. The 2-ball will follow the 1-ball into the same pocket. Trick shot artist, George Middleditch, executes this shot to perfection.

STEADY, STEADY!!

For this trick, you need three cues with the same size tips. Place the cue ball against the two cues laying flat on the table. Take the third cue, using it to push under the cue ball (very slowly) until the cue tip meets the other two tips. Now, the cue ball should be resting on the top of the three cue tips. Keeping the tips of the cues together, raise the cue ball above the table high enough (about 3 or 4 feet) in order to place the third cue under the cushion. Now all three cues should be locked into place with the cue ball still resting in the middle of the tips about 3 or 4 feet above the bed of the table.

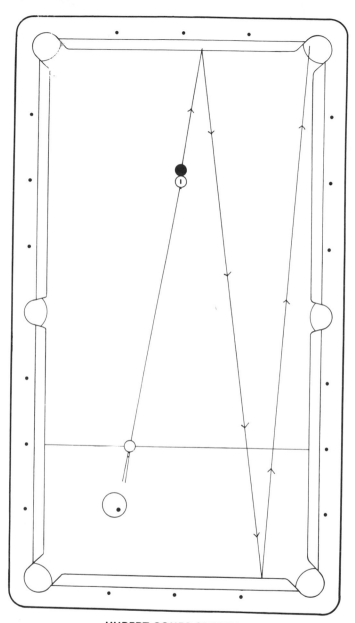

HUBERT COKES SPECIAL
Be sure the two object balls are frozen. Aim to hit the front ball head on (maybe a fraction left of center). Stroke the cue ball hard with low right English. The back ball should bank two rails into the corner pocket. Often, this shot comes up in a game of one pocket. Hubert Cokes taught me this shot. Many say Hubert invented the game of one-pocket. Hubert taught me the game of one-pocket and was a very good friend of mine.

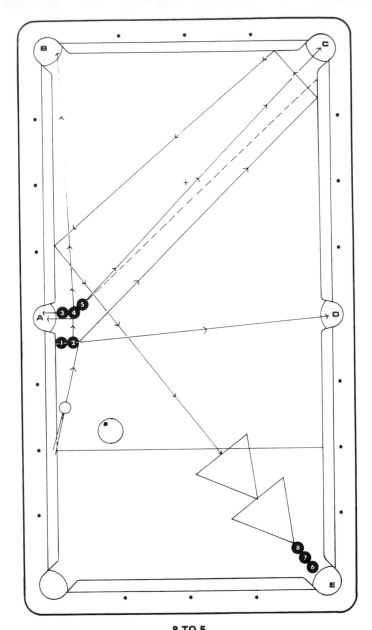

8 TO 5

This trick shot is similar to the one used on the Miller Lite commercial. Line up the 5-ball along the dotted line. Aim to hit the 2-ball about ⅓ to ¼ full. The cue ball will circle the table and hit the first triangle to pocket the other three balls. You like to show off . . . right!

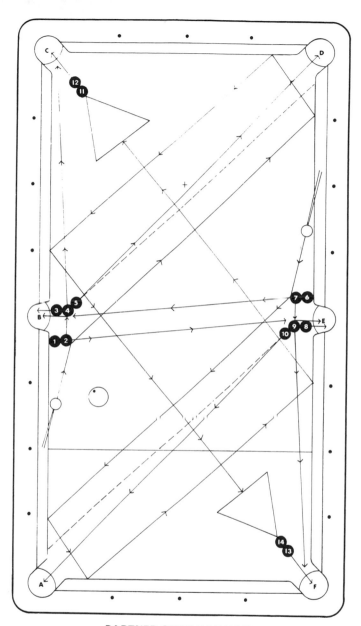

PARTNER SHOT (14 BALLS)

Get yourself a good partner for this shot. Set-up is very similar to the preceding shot (8 balls -5 pockets). Both players must practice their timing on this shot so they will shoot at the same time. Otherwise, it won't work! Each player should hit the cue ball firmly and with high left English. Aim to hit the 2-ball and 7-ball ⅓ to ¼ full. Be sure the 12-ball and 13-ball are far enough from the rail in order to allow the 4-ball and 9-ball to pass without moving them.

137

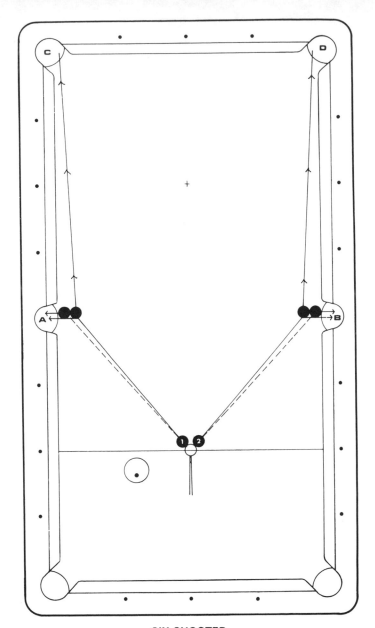

SIX SHOOTER

Line up the 1-ball and the 2-ball along the dotted lines. Aim at the center of the table. Hit the cue ball firmly. Don't be too disappointed if this trick doesn't go on the first try.

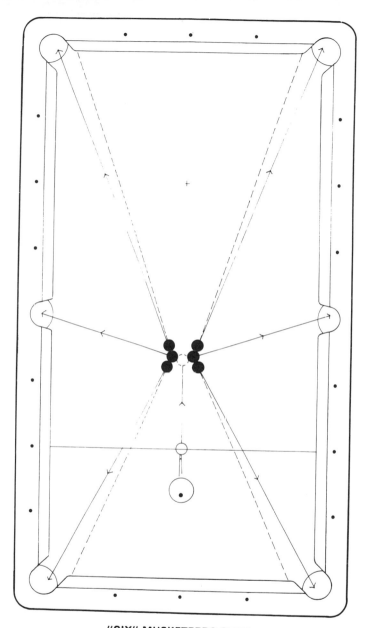

"SIX" MUSKETEERS SHOT

Line up the four balls along the dotted lines. Notice the two middle balls are above the diamonds toward the side pockets. Aim the cue ball to split the two middle balls and hit the cue ball with a firm stroke. Watch all six balls disappear into the pockets . . . all for one and one for all . . . Be ready to soak up the applause!

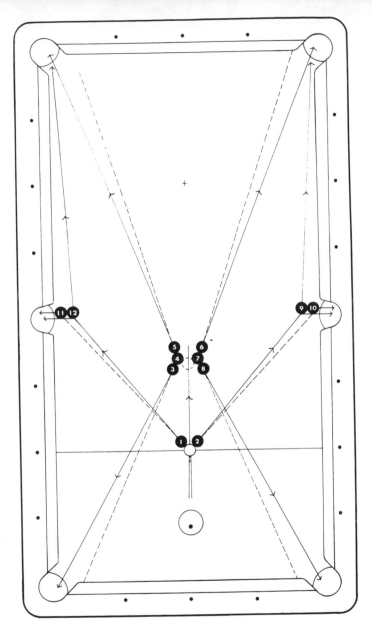

"HIGH NOON"

Truly a sensational trick shot -- a combination of the two preceding 6-ball shots. Set-up and a good stroke are essential. The cue ball is on the spot. Once you learn to make the two 6-ball shots, combining them into a 12-ball shot is a natural. Hit the cue ball extra-firm on this shot.

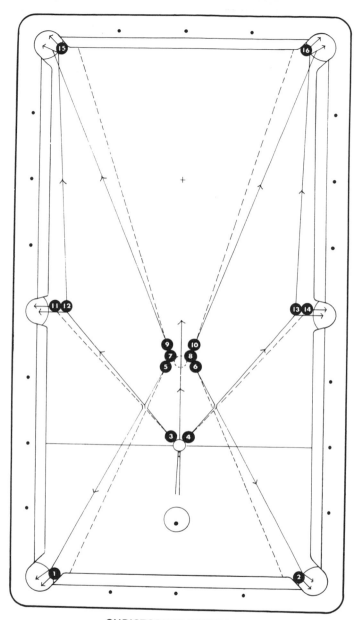

CHRISTOPHER NICHOLAS

Our old friend, the 12-ball shot, but with the addition of four balls placed on the side edges of the corner pockets. One of the toughest to make, hit the cue ball with a hard stroke. After making this shot, your friends will think that you can do anything! I named the shot after my son who was 16 days late.

Professional Tournament Championships

Indianapolis 9-Ball Open
Minnesota Fats Challenge Match, Evansville
Midwest Open 9-Ball, Galesburg, IL
Midwest Open 14.1 (BCA), Rockford, IL
Texas Open 14.1 (BCA), Austin, TX
KY State Open 14.1 (BCA), Owensboro, KY
World Open 14.1 (PPPA), New York
BCA National 8-Ball Champion, Columbus, OH
Kentucky Derby Open 9-Ball, Louisville, KY
Illinois 9-Ball Open, Decatur, IL
BCA 8-Ball Qualifier, Russellville, KY
Kentucky Open 9-Ball, Bowling Green, KY
World 9-Ball Championship (PPPA), Atlantic City
Kentucky Open 9-Ball, Bowling Green, KY
Bowling Green Open (Bank), Bowling Green, KY
Prestonburg Open 9-Ball, Prestonburg, KY
Bowling Green Open 9-Ball, Bowling Green, KY
Owensboro Open 9-Ball, Owensboro, KY
McDermott Masters Champion 9-Ball, Milwaukee
San Jose Open 9-Ball, San Jose, CA
Kentucky Open 9-Ball, Bowling Green, KY
National Open 9-Ball, Indianapolis, IN
Kentucky Open 9-Ball, Bowling Green, KY
Fresno Open 9-Ball, Fresno, CA
Tennessee State 9-Ball Open, Chattanooga, TN
Zurich Open 9-Ball, Zurich, Switzerland
World Open Champion 14.1 (PPPA), Philadelphia
Charlotte Open 9-Ball, Charlotte, NC
Sacramento Open 9-Ball, Sacramento, CA
Midwest Open 9-Ball, Madison, WI
Kentucky Open 9-Ball, Elizabethtown, KY
McDermott Masters 9-Ball, Davenport, IA
Glass City Open 9-Ball, Toledo, OH
Scranton Invitational 9-Ball, Scranton, PA
Tennessee State 9-Ball Open, Chattanooga, TN
Sands Regent 9-Ball Open, Reno, NV
Rakm Up 9-Ball Classic, Columbia, SC
Knoxville 9-Ball Open, Knoxville, TN
Governors Cup 9-Ball, Columbus, OH
Glass City Open 9-Ball, Toledo, OH
Sands Regent 9-Ball Open, Reno, NV
MPBA Brunswick World Championship, Las Vegas
Golden 8-Ball Invitational, Phoenix, AZ
Scranton Open 9-Ball, Scranton, PA
Lexington All Star Open, Lexington, KY
Akron Open 9-Ball, Akron, OH
U. S. Open 9-Ball, Norfolk, VA
9-Ball Billiard World Series Champion, Manila
Challenge Match Nick Varner vs. Efren Reyes
Al Romero Classic 9-Ball, Los Angeles, CA
U. S. Open 9-Ball, Norfolk, VA
West End All Around Shoot Out, Elizabeth, NJ
(9-Ball, 14.1, One Pocket)
Rakm Up 9-Ball Classic, Columbia, SC
Super Bowl XXVI Billiard Champion, Minneapolis, MN
International One Pocket Champion, Washington, DC